MORE THAN PETTICOATS SERIES

More Than PETTICOATS

REMARKABLE CALIFORNIA WOMEN

Erin H. Turner

TWODOT®

GUILFORD, CONNECTICUT
HELENA, MONTANA
AN IMPRINT OF THE GLOBE PEQUOT PRESS

D0189944

A · T W O D O T · B O O K

Copyright © 1999 Morris Book Publishing, LLC

TwoDot is a registered trademark of Morris Book Publishing, LLC.

Cover photo: Two women in front of Yosemite Falls. Courtesy of Yosemite Research Library.

Library of Congress Cataloging-in-Publication Data

Turner, Erin H., 1973-
    More than petticoats : remarkable California women / Erin H. Turner.
      p. cm.
    Includes bibliographical references and index.
    ISBN 978-1-56044-859-4 (pbk.)
    1. Women—California Biography. 2. California Biography.
  I. Title.
  CT3260.T87 1999
  920.72'09794—dc21   99-27234
                                                     CIP

Manufactured in the United States of America
First Edition/Fifth Printing

ACKNOWLEDGMENTS

I would like to thank a number of people who helped me put together this manuscript and who have been my support during this process. First, I must commend my talented editor, Megan Hiller, and Charlene Patterson, who was responsible for the photo acquisitions. Next, I have to thank my unflappable husband, Ross, for graciously putting up with yet another round of, "Do you know what I learned todays?" Notes and well-wishes from my mentor and professor Victoria Brown kept me fired up, and her classes on U.S. women's history and on biography were often in my mind as I worked. The kind folks at the information desk at the Lewis and Clark Public Library came to my rescue with tall piles of interlibrary loan materials, and I recommend that anyone who wants to know more about women's history visit the National Women's History Project website at www.nwhp.org.

I must also thank my family, and especially my mother, grandmothers, aunts, and sister, for providing me with daily examples of remarkable womanhood and for telling me tales of their mothers and grandmothers. My mother first pointed me toward the biography section of the library when I was still in elementary school, and though I didn't quite get through all the books about Eisenhower and Lincoln, I read Julia Ward Howe, Jane Addams, Elizabeth Cady Stanton, Susan B. Anthony, Dorothea Dix, and others dozens of times. For that I will always be grateful.

Contents

*I*NTRODUCTION

"*I*f she had only been a man" are words that have been used and overused to start or finish many musings about a woman's accomplishments. Said by men and women alike, they exemplify a time in the history of the world—a time that has not ended in some places—when simply being the smartest, the bravest, the wittiest, or the best was not enough to guarantee a place on the bench or in the office or behind the controls. The words are still said today, perhaps with less frequency, but they point to a basic, blatant discrimination that has existed in the separation of men and women's lives into two different spheres. They were likely said of the women in this book during their lifetimes and even after.

For a long time in history books, and even in women's history books, the women who were reported as examples of remarkable womanhood were the few who undertook to become lawyers or doctors when there were no other women doing such a thing. It was remarkable for a woman before the middle of the twentieth century to take on a traditionally male role. But women who stretched the boundaries of their own sphere or reinvented it without assuming a male role are equally remarkable—and on their accomplishments we should place at least as much value. In addition, we should also value and recognize the community of women that helped them take on those roles in what was frequently not an isolated act of bravery.

As the twentieth century comes to a close, it seems fitting to look back at the accomplishments of women during the last hundred years. Now, more than ever, women can be found in almost every domain once thought to be man's alone. Women fill the ranks of professions such as architecture, medicine, the law, telecommunications, publishing, finance, and more. They are factory workers, supervisors, combat pilots, contractors, and mechanics. In the United States, we've had a female secretary of state, two female justices on the Supreme Court, and numerous female senators and representatives at the federal and state levels; and there are stirrings of women presidential candidates in the 2000 elections. And it has only been eighty short years since women's suffrage became law.

It is also interesting to look back and see the many accomplishments that can be attributed to women who lived in a time before feminism was in vogue and then went out of fashion, before the right to vote was won, and before the twentieth century became the here and now, and not the future to be. Victoria Claflin Woodhull, a notorious figure whose name recognition has soared in recent years, was actually the first woman to run for president, in 1872. A short-time California resident, she was a stockbroker in New York City before her nomination by the Equal Rights Party, and she had what were considered dangerous thoughts on equality in marriage, among other things. Her daring was a benchmark in the struggles of nineteenth-century women to earn the vote, and she was joined by many others—Susan B. Anthony, Elizabeth Cady Stanton, and Frances Willard, among them—who took up the cause of women's rights as a righteous cause. Surely she was a remarkable woman among remarkable women.

The ten women featured in this book, all born before 1900, all remarkable in their own way, were at least partially responsible for propelling the cause of women into the twentieth century or carrying it through its early years—whether this was their intention or not. It is unlikely that many of them thought of themselves as activists; if they did, it is likely they thought their activism was focused in directions other than toward women's rights. Included here are a powerful, wealthy businesswoman, two writers, two interpreters, a tour guide, an architect of sorts, a photographer, an artist, and an actress—all of whom made a difference for women in ways large and small. Mary Ellen Pleasant knew she was an abolitionist but might not have included women's rights among her causes. Sarah Winchester's cause was of an entirely different sort, but in working for it she certainly stretched the boundaries of possibility for women.

What these women are not are women who would have been great if they had been men, or who were remarkable only because they took on roles that traditionally fell outside the boundaries of what was proper for women of the era to do—though some of them certainly did, others did not. It is important to note when writing or reading about pioneer and Native American women of the 1800s and early 1900s that simply managing day-to-day survival was often remarkable. The same is true of immigrants to this country, and, particularly in California, of the thousands of Japanese who were interned in prison camps during World War II. While this statement is true of men on the frontier and in a new country as well, women faced special obstacles on the frontier—including the universal problems and joys of pregnancy and motherhood, and, in some cases, having little or no choice in shaping the destiny determined by their husbands' wanderlust.

Therefore, this is by no means a complete history of all of the remarkable women in California. Starting with the native women who practiced basketweaving as an art, continuing on to the Spanish women who helped settle the area when it was part of Mexico, including the women who emigrated to the area in the mid-1800s, and following the history of California women who worked in the twentieth-century war plants, and finishing with those who live and work in the state today—what isn't remarkable? California itself is a land of challenges and opportunities that women continue to accept every day.

INTRODUCTION

In choosing the ten women who are presented in this book, I left out a good many whose stories are also fascinating. Juana Briones was an early resident of the town of Yerba Buena, which would become known as San Francisco, and worked as a doctor and a rancher in the mid-1800s. Julia Morgan was a San Francisco architect in the first half of the twentieth century who designed Hearst Castle and other famous buildings. Julia B. Platt was an embryologist and neuroscientist at the turn of the century. Rosa Smith Eigenmann was the first female ichthyologist in the United States when she began her work in the late 1800s. Their stories are just a few among so many that could be included here.

Remarkable women have never existed in a vacuum. A community of strong women—mothers, grandmothers, sisters, and others—frequently surround and support each other. Excellent examples of this are Mary Pickford's friendship with Frances Marion, an early screenwriter who got her start as the first female war correspondent in World War I, and Tye Leung Schulze, who got her start as an activist from a woman named Donaldina Cameron who ran a mission home for Chinese girls in San Francisco. Tye also worked side-by-side with women like Katherine Maurer, a deaconess in the United Methodist Church who worked tirelessly with immigrants at the Angel Island Immigration Station in San Francisco Bay. Florence Hutchings was part of a large group of women who worked and played in Yosemite National Park in its earliest days, including her grandmother, Florantha Sproat, a fearless mountain climber and fine cook.

It has been said that women's history is an untold part of the American experience. While that is certainly true, in recent years there has been an amazing upswing of interest in the history of women in the United States. To a large extent, the stories are no longer untold, but it is time to stop putting too much emphasis on what could have been if only these women had been allowed to behave as men would in a man's world. The women who were chosen for this book are remarkable *because* they were women, not in spite of it. Their womanhood informed their choices and defined the narrow sphere in which they lived, worked, and were able to effect change. Their femininity, or their utter lack of it in some cases, defined them. They didn't have to be men or even take on a male profession in order to realize their full potential as human beings and as history makers. They were remarkable and a part of a remarkable community in California. ✤

Mary Ellen Pleasant
1814–1904

A Whole Theatre to Herself

On May 7, 1899, Mrs. Teresa Bell quietly sat and wrote in her diary as her mind raced with possibilities. Deliberately and carefully, she made a strange and cryptic note about a night seven years previous at her spacious mansion on Octavia Street in San Francisco. Her husband, Thomas Bell, a successful San Francisco businessman, had died mysteriously in the house that night. Only his son Fred, the servants, and Mary Ellen Pleasant, a woman variously described as the housekeeper and Thomas Bell's business partner—when she wasn't being referred to with veiled innuendoes as his mistress or in cruder terms—were present. Teresa Bell had been at her ranch house in Sonoma County at the time of the accident, but her carefully crafted diary entry said that Fred Bell had given her new information about her husband's death—naming Mary Ellen Pleasant as the culprit in what Teresa Bell claimed had only appeared to be accidental.

Nearly everyone in San Francisco assumed that Thomas Bell had died on October 15, 1892, following a fall from the stairway in his mansion when, after an illness, he had arisen in the night and stumbled about. Most people believed that the servants had discovered his crumpled body on the cold, hard basement floor twenty feet below after hearing his cries and that Fred and Mary Ellen Pleasant had been summoned to his side immediately. Seven years later, Bell's widow, Teresa, laid the groundwork for a strange tale about her husband's violent death in her diary, and after Mary Ellen Pleasant's death in 1904, she tried to be sure that everyone knew the gruesome details of that October night.

In 1904, Teresa Bell expanded the note in her diary with a bizarre and frightening tale about the events that surrounded her husband's death. She claimed that on the night he died, he had fallen from the stairs but did not expire until twenty minutes later when he was in Mary Ellen Pleasant's presence. Teresa Bell elaborated her tale, saying that Mary Ellen Pleasant had "put her fingers in the hole in the top of his head and pulled out the protruding brains. . . ." It was a strange and macabre story, which, when Mrs. Bell published it, forever solidified the legend of Mary Ellen Pleasant.

Mary Ellen Pleasant was a strange woman for her time, because it was unheard of for a woman to stand up to authority or to challenge society's norms. Her strangeness made her legendary, and when someone is legendary, the facts are often hard to discern from the myths that surround their lives. In fact, she was a phenomenally successful businesswoman with interests all over San Francisco and throughout California, and her rise to these heights through her own work was a remarkable story. Her story was especially strange, however, because she wasn't a white woman of privilege, but a black woman who devised her own means to power.

Mary Ellen Pleasant claimed that she was born to free parents in the segregated city of Philadelphia, Pennsylvania, on August 19, 1814. The mysteries about her early life are nearly as clouded as those from her infamous years in San Francisco, as she herself was close-mouthed and aloof. According to legend, her father may or

Mary Ellen Pleasant at 87 years of age.

may not have been white, and some even suggested he was a Southern slaveholder. Others claimed that he was a Cherokee Indian or a Kanaka—a native from Polynesia. Who her father was is unknown, but it is likely that he was a freedman living in the North when his daughter was born. Her mother was most likely a black woman—presumably a former slave—from Louisiana.

As a young girl, Mary Ellen Pleasant went to Nantucket, Massachusetts, to live with a Quaker family to be educated. Perhaps her family believed that the Quakers' belief in equality of the races would mean a better life for their daughter than they could offer her in their segregated city. Unfortunately, the family she was sent to kept the money that was to be used for the education and, instead, sent her to work. Mary Ellen Pleasant left Nantucket and returned to Philadelphia when she was about fourteen or fifteen, and she always regretted her lack of formal education.

Though she was poor and without formal training, an important first step toward the life she was to lead did begin in Philadelphia. There, she met and married a wealthy black man named James Henry Smith. The couple became deeply involved in the fight to abolish slavery that was fomenting throughout the nation in the years prior to the Civil War, and they were fervent supporters of the Underground Railroad, the route by which escaped slaves from the South made their way to safety in Canada. After they had been married a few years, James Smith died, leaving Mary Ellen Pleasant a substantial fortune, and she continued with the work the couple had started.

In 1848, she married a former slave named John James Pleasant, and not much more is known about her second husband than about the first. Perhaps even in her thirties, before she gained much of her wealth and power, Mary Ellen Pleasant's life had already evolved into a one-woman show. She said of herself in later years, "I am a whole theatre to myself." By the time she met her second husband, she was already a woman capable of taking on any role and of taking on anyone who stood in her way.

Sometime between 1848 and 1852, the Pleasants emigrated to the West, following the paths of many black and white abolitionists from Philadelphia. They settled in San Francisco in the new state of California, and Mary Ellen Pleasant made a living working as a housekeeper in the homes of several of the city's wealthiest and most powerful men. She made several very wise investments with her first husband's fortune during these years, gleaning information about the best way to increase her wealth through careful listening during the lavish dinner parties she oversaw. By 1855, she had amassed quite a sum and was the owner of several San Francisco laundries. She was also the holder of enough secrets—gleaned from years of careful watching and listening—to make her a powerful force to be reckoned with, and perhaps even a woman to fear.

This shrewd businesswoman could have been one of the wealthiest people in Calfornia if she had been interested in making money; for her, though, money was but a means to an end. She gave it away almost as soon as she got it, for the most part using it to bring freedmen and fugitive slaves to California and to help them get on their feet once there. Her philanthropy was extensive, and she exercised considerable political clout as well. It was probably due to Mary Ellen Pleasant's support that a California law forbidding black testimony in a court of law was repealed.

People who tried to stand in the way of what Mary Ellen Pleasant might have termed "progress" certainly knew it after the fact. In October 1866, she tried to take a seat on a San Francisco streetcar, and the driver ordered her to leave his vehicle. Clearly the driver did not know who he was dealing with, for if he had he would have saved himself and the bus company a great deal of trouble. To him, the tall, stately black woman looked like just another former slave, one of many who had fled to California seeking opportunity after the Civil War, and he ordered her off the steps just as he would have done to any other black who approached his car. Perhaps he didn't notice that she was as finely dressed as any of the white women he picked up on his regular route. He probably didn't notice the anger that flashed in the woman's eyes, either.

On October 18, 1866, the front page of the *Alta California* carried the story of Mrs. Pleasant's failed ride. The paper reported:

> Mrs. Mary E. Pleasants, a woman of color, having complained of the driver of car No. 6 of the Omnibus Railroad Company's line, for putting her off the car, appeared yesterday in the Police Court and withdrew the charge, stating as a reason for doing so that she had been informed by the agents of the Company that negroes would hearafter be allowed to ride on the car, let the effect on the Company's business be what it might.

Shortly after the incident on the streetcar, Mrs. Pleasant, a widow again after the death of her second husband, formed an alliance with multimillionaire Thomas Bell, a cofounder of the Bank of California. No one knows what the true nature of their relationship was beyond business, but business partners they were, and a great deal of mutual respect existed between them. In 1879, Mary Ellen Pleasant introduced Thomas Bell to Teresa Percy. Thomas and Teresa were married and in a few months all three had moved into a fabulous mansion on the corner of Octavia and Bush Streets built to Mrs. Pleasant's specifications.

Perhaps most people preferred to think that Mary Ellen Pleasant—sometimes disrespectfully called Mammy Pleasant, much to her dismay—was, in fact, the housekeeper. No doubt, she did act as an executive in that role, hiring and firing servants, and buying groceries, but she was much more. Mary Ellen Pleasant handled all of

Teresa's financial needs, acting as mediator between husband and wife. She also chose Teresa's clothes, friends, and activities.

People all over town wondered at their odd relationship, but Mrs. Pleasant was unlikely to satisfy them. Once she told a judge, "Mr. Bell knew what I was there for, and I knew what I was there for." No more would she say.

The strangeness of the relationship seemed to overshadow the good that Mrs. Pleasant was doing around the city, and all kinds of rumors pervaded the general atmosphere of mystery that shrouded the mansion. Stories that Mary Ellen Pleasant trafficked in prostitutes, engaged in the practice of voodoo, and bought and sold babies ran rampant all over town, even before Thomas Bell's death. By the late 1890s, after Thomas Bell's death and even after she and Teresa had stopped sharing the Octavia Street residence, the legend that was Mary Ellen Pleasant's life had found its way into the common history of San Francisco.

In fact, it was the break with Teresa Bell, widow of the man who had been her business partner, that precipitated the growth of the legend of Mary Ellen Pleasant's life. After her husband's death, Teresa Bell turned with anger against the woman who had been her sole support for almost ten years. She threw Mary Ellen Pleasant out of the mansion and conspired with a newspaper reporter to spread the stories of voodoo and prostitution, which were all too eagerly read by a public who wanted a reason for Mrs. Pleasant's success. Teresa also bought interest in a popular magazine that had planned to publish Mary Ellen Pleasant's memoirs, ruling out any chance that Mrs. Pleasant's side of the story could be heard, and managed to steal many of Mrs. Pleasant's other important documents. All the while, she wrote quietly in her diary of the terrible things that Mary Ellen Pleasant had done, and then gave her volumes to a San Francisco newspaperman after Mrs. Pleasant's death in 1904.

Perhaps Teresa Bell was worried about what Mary Ellen Pleasant might do to her if the story was revealed before Mrs. Pleasant was beyond her power to injure her. Still, there is strong evidence that suggests that Teresa Bell went completely mad before she began her campaign to ruin Mary Ellen Pleasant. Teresa's own children had her declared incompetent because, among other things, she claimed she could float through the air, and that she had, in fact, floated over New York City. Teresa also claimed that she could light the gaslights without a match, just by waving her hand. These same children staunchly supported Mary Ellen Pleasant's claim that the Octavia Street house and many of its furnishings and the jewels claimed by Teresa Bell, were actually hers.

Some historians say that the diaries that were concocted to ruin Mary Ellen Pleasant were much more injurious to Teresa Bell, in that they show what a demented state of mind the woman was in when she made her accusations against a woman who had really done more good for the city of San Francisco and for its less fortunate inhabitants than almost anyone else. As for the murder of Thomas Bell, the *San Francisco Chronicle* reported the story much differently in the days after the incident than Teresa Bell would in her diary.

According to the *Chronicle*, it was about half-past ten on the night of October 15, 1892, when the servants at the mansion on Octavia Street heard the cries of Thomas Bell, and a dull thud after his body had fallen the twenty feet from stair railing to basement floor. They immediately ran to awaken his son and Mary Ellen Pleasant. The story reported that when Mrs. Pleasant and Thomas Bell's son Fred reached the body, she:

> detected signs of life, however, and busied herself with procuring pillows and blankets, while Fred Bell ran for Dr. Murphy, the nearest physician. Dr. Kearney of 513

Folsom Street, who has been attending Mr. Bell was telephoned for also, and he arrived a few minutes after Dr. Murphy had the unconscious man carried back to his bedroom.

The two physicians first directed their attention to rousing Mr. Bell from his deep stupor, but all the resources at hand failed and they devoted themselves to a diagnosis of his injuries. Concussion of the brain was apparent but no fracture of the skull could be discovered. . . .

The *San Francisco Examiner* told a similar tale with Mary Ellen Pleasant's testimony. It recounted Mrs. Pleasant's words:

Mr. Bell had been ailing for about two months now, and has been in bed since last Monday. He was badly run down, the doctor said, and besides he had a trouble of the skin that just kept him in torture. Twenty minutes before 10 o'clock last night he got up without calling anyone and went to the bathroom which is close to his chamber on the upper floor. . . . From there he must have started to go downstairs. There are two winding flights leading from the upper story to the kitchen, and at the bottom of the top flight we found the blanket which I always left on the foot of the bed for him to throw over his shoulders when he arose in the night.

She went on to say that he must have become disoriented when he arose and taken a spill over the railing. Fred Bell confirmed her story, and the coroner agreed that it had been an accidental death.

Still, the rumors that Teresa Bell started about Mary Ellen Pleasant would be accepted readily and over the years became solidified in the public mind as fact. In truth, there was a great deal about Mrs. Pleasant that was unknown, and perhaps because of her successes in a time when being a woman, and what was more, being black, should have kept her from any role above that of housewife or domestic servant, it might have been easier for people to believe that it was voodoo or illegal practice that made her a success.

Many people who knew her described Mary Ellen Pleasant as a formidable, terrifying woman. Others have said after reviewing her story and meeting her, "[If she] had been white and a man, she would have been president," and "Even as a woman she might have commanded an army successfully." She certainly proved that regardless of your sex or race you could be a success, and she used her success to better the situation of others. Whether the public record of her good deeds or the private, then public, musings of Teresa Bell are correct, Mary Ellen Pleasant was one of the most amazing and remarkable people in California. Her life was of the stuff that makes for good fiction, and it will probably never be reconciled with fact. ✤

Jessie Benton Frémont
1824–1902

Pioneer with a Pen

*W*hen eighteen-year-old Jessie Benton Frémont returned home from a long walk through the streets of St. Louis, Missouri, in the spring of 1843, a pile of mail that required her immediate attention was waiting. On top of the stack of correspondence was a long, official-looking envelope addressed to her husband, John Charles Frémont, and she wasted no time in opening it. Since the small Frémont family—Jessie, John Charles, and their infant daughter, Lily—had come to the then far-western outpost of St. Louis from Washington, D.C., Jessie had acted as secretary for her lieutenant husband and the expedition he was preparing for to explore a route to the Oregon Territory.

When the letter arrived, John Charles was in Westport Landing (near what is now Kansas City), a few days' journey from St. Louis. After Jessie quickly scanned the contents of the envelope from Washington, she knew just what to do, and she wasted no time. Jessie hurriedly sent for a man named de Rosier, who was a French Canadian planning to join the Frémont expedition in a few days. She told him, "An important letter has come for Lieutenant

Frémont, and I want it delivered without loss of time. How long will you need to get ready?"

De Rosier replied that he only needed the time to get his horse, and Jessie continued that she wanted him to say nothing of the letter to anyone else, and that she wanted him to take it because on horseback he could avoid the loss of time that mail boats faced on bends in the river. De Rosier offered to take his brother along to help speed the journey and to bring back an answer.

When de Rosier went for his brother to prepare him, Jessie sat at her desk to write John Charles a note; she didn't plan to forward the letter, but instead to write one of her own. She directed her husband, "Do not lose a day, but start at once. I cannot tell you the reason, but you must GO. Only trust me and go." The official letter from Washington would not make it into her husband's hands nor be seen by anyone but Jessie herself.

A week went by, and Jessie had heard nothing. But, at last, de Rosier's brother arrived at her door with a note from her husband. It said only, "Goodbye. I trust and go."

John Charles Frémont was safely on his way west to explore an overland route to the Oregon Territory. With her quick thinking and the fast work of her pen, Jessie had possibly changed her own destiny, that of her explorer husband, and perhaps even that of the thousands of people who would follow him west.

In spite of her rather sheltered upbringing, or perhaps because of it, Jessie was ideally suited to the task she took upon herself that day in St. Louis. Jessie Benton was born on May 31, 1824, at her mother's family plantation in Virginia, called Cherry Grove. She was the second of five children, with one older sister, one younger sister, and two younger brothers. Her mother's family were wealthy Virginia planters, and her mother had been a Southern belle. Jessie's father's family came from the far western state of Missouri, where

Jessie Benton Frémont

her grandmother lived in St. Louis when Jessie was a child. Jessie's father, Thomas Hart Benton, was one of Missouri's most famous citizens and a senator from that state.

When Jessie was a child, the Benton family split their time between three homes, Cherry Grove, St. Louis, and Washington, D.C. In the winter, they lived in Washington while Congress was in session; in even-numbered years they would make the short journey to Cherry Grove for the summer, and in odd-numbered years they would make the longer trip to St. Louis for the summer since Congress recessed earlier in those years.

During the summers, the Benton children were encouraged to play outside and exercise a great deal, and Jessie grew up healthy and robust. Winter was her favorite time, however, because although she had to spend time studying with tutors, she was also able to spend time with her father in his study, where she learned a great deal more than her school books or tutors could teach her. As she grew older, she and her older sister, Eliza, helped their father entertain many important Washington guests, because their mother was frequently ill.

Perhaps because of her extraordinary educational opportunities and her father's encouragement, Jessie became headstrong and matured early in spite of the tendency in that day to encourage girls to be ornamental, but not intelligent and well-spoken. She was actually considered quite a beauty, however, with a lovely oval face, curly red-brown hair, and large, dark eyes; by the time she was fourteen, she had received two proposals of marriage.

At about that time, her parents decided that Jessie needed the influence of a finishing school for young ladies to teach her the skills expected of a demure Southern belle, and to keep her from the reach of eligible Washington bachelors. They decided to send her and her older sister to Miss English's Select Academy.

Jessie was devastated at the thought of going away to a girls' school. Her happiest times were spent with her father in his comfortable office in their large brick home in Washington. Rather than accept the decree without a fight, she took a pair of scissors and cut off all of her beautiful hair because she thought her parents would be too embarrassed to send her to Miss English's that way. She thought wrong and was bundled off to the academy with Eliza.

Jessie claimed that while she was at Miss English's, she didn't learn much, but she made many friends. One of her closest chums was a young woman named Harriet Beall Williams. Harriet was also a beautiful young girl, and at the age of sixteen, she married a Russian count—Alexander de la Bodisco—who was sixty-one years old. Jessie was first bridesmaid at the wedding, and though she was disappointed with the age of her friend's new husband, the romance of the wedding sparked her imagination.

In the spring after Harriet's wedding, Eliza and Jessie's younger sister, Sarah, came to visit them at the academy to attend a concert. Accompanying her was a young stranger in uniform who had become a close friend of the Bentons during the time Eliza and Jessie were at school. The dashing soldier's name was John Charles Frémont, and Jessie fell in love with him at first sight.

When Jessie met John Charles, he was a second lieutenant in the U.S. Topographical Corps, and he had already made one expedition west to the Mississippi River. When he returned to Washington to write the official report of the expedition, he had met Thomas Hart Benton, Jessie's father.

Within a few short months, sixteen-year-old Jessie and the twenty-seven-year-old John Charles became secretly engaged to be married. It was secret because, while her family liked John Charles, they didn't approve of their daughter marrying a man who had no family, no money, and who would probably have to spend his life traveling far from Jessie's side. Eventually, the Bentons found out about the engagement, and Thomas Hart Benton was able to arrange for John Charles to be assigned to a distant expedition. He thought that if he could persuade Jessie to wait to marry John Charles, during his long absence she might change her mind.

However, when John Charles returned to a thoroughly miserable Jessie after his trip to the West, she was unchanged in her feelings and so was he. Benton still forbade the marriage and insisted that they wait at least six more months before making such a commitment.

Willful, headstrong Jessie found a way to marry her dashing hero, however, in secret on October 19, 1841. She was only seventeen, and he was twenty-eight. Jessie's adventures were just beginning.

Thomas Hart Benton was furious when he learned the news, but John Charles moved into the Benton's Washington mansion to prepare for his next expedition and Thomas Hart Benton became his staunchest supporter. Then came the first trip west to explore the overland route to the Oregon Territory.

John Charles was gone for the entire summer following the couple's marriage, and Jessie was already pregnant. She delivered a daughter on November 13, 1842, shortly after John Charles's return. Jessie was busy with the new baby, Lily, but in time her husband needed her as well. He had returned to write his report of his trip westward, but every time he sat down to complete it, he felt unable. Nosebleeds, migraine headaches, and severe writer's block would stop him.

Jessie was anxious for her husband to complete the report quickly, so she offered a solution. He could describe the journey to her, and she could transcribe his thoughts. Thus Jessie made her first cross-country journey through her husband's words and descriptions, as she frantically raced her pen across the page to keep up.

The report that John Charles and Jessie completed together was regarded the first, best, and most accurate report on the West, and it encouraged many emigrants to undertake the long journey to Oregon. It also solidified John Charles's reputation as a leader and an explorer, and soon he was asked to undertake his next journey, all the way to the West Coast.

This time, Jessie went along as far as St. Louis, her childhood summer home, taking the baby. John Charles would be stationed at Westport Landing until he could ready the expedition. Jessie would stay in St. Louis and handle correspondence and other tasks.

During the preparations for the expedition, John Charles ordered and received a twelve-pound cannon, but the captain at the arsenal that provided it wrote a letter to Washington stating his disapproval. It was the response to this letter that Jessie found after her walk that warm summer day. In the letter, Colonel Abert of the Bureau of Engineers questioned the need for the cannon, and wanted John Charles to delay the expedition and return to Washington to answer for its necessity. Jessie knew that unless he started out immediately, the expedition would be delayed indefinitely. She acted swiftly and later said:

> I was only eighteen, an age when one takes risks willingly. I felt the whole situation in a flash, and met it—as I saw right. I had been too much a part of the whole plan for the expeditions to put them in peril now—and I alone could act.

Jessie had several long years to wait before she and John Charles would actually be together for any length of time. When he left in the spring of 1843 at her urging, he would be gone for more than a year and a half. When he returned, Jessie again helped him write the report, and surely her curiosity grew to see the lands of which he spoke. After being home for nine months, John Charles left again, and this time he would be gone for two years. Most of his journey was spent in California, where the Mexican-American War started in 1846 after a revolt in Sonoma, partially at John Charles's urging. During the journey, John Charles gave a friend some money to buy property along the coast in California, hoping to return with Jessie and the baby.

Tragedy struck when John Charles was forced to return to the United States to be court-martialed. Shortly after California gained its independence in 1848 and was made a territory of the United States, there was a dispute over who should be the territorial governor. One military commander appointed John Charles Frémont. Another, John Charles's commanding officer, did not agree and found that John Charles was in direct violation of his order when he refused to step down, an offense for which he could be court-martialed or even charged with mutiny.

John Charles returned to Washington with Jessie for the trial and was eventually found guilty, but President Polk pardoned him. Though he was no longer Lieutenant Frémont, John Charles and Jessie would finally have a chance for a family life together, and they chose to go to California to live on the land he had purchased. John Charles set out first to make it livable for his little family, with Jessie to follow.

In 1849, when Jessie was finally able to travel to California, she had three choices of how to make the trip. She could either make the overland trip in a covered wagon, taking upwards of three months, sail on a ship around the southern tip of South America, which could take even longer, or take a ship to the Isthmus of Panama, cross the strip of land there, and continue by boat to San Francisco, where John Charles would be waiting. Jessie chose the third option for her journey, and with little Lily in tow she set out from New York in a steamship and traveled over the isthmus on small boats

General Frémont, wife and daughter, and a party of thirteen, showing the circumference of the Giant after encircling the tree.

and canoes down the Chagres River. Though it took only a month, it was a dangerous trip, and many travelers who chose that way died en route, but Lily and Jessie made it safely to the waters of the Pacific on the other side of the jungle.

Throngs of fortune seekers who were searching for deposits of gold in the wake of a small find in the South Fork of the American River were also arriving in San Francisco when Lily and Jessie stepped off the boat. John Charles surprised Jessie with the news that gold had, in fact, been found on his ranch, named the Mariposas, and that he already had crews working to bring the precious ore up to the surface. Jessie, once a poor explorer's wife, was now the wife of a wealthy gold miner. Their luck had certainly changed.

Almost as soon as Jessie began to settle into her new home, while John Charles worked at the mines, a convention was called in Monterey to determine the future of California as a state. Mexico had ceded the territory to the United States after the Mexican-American War, but it was still run as a military territory. Citizens of

California were gathering to elect representatives to be sent to Washington, D.C.

Jessie was thrilled! She loved politics as a girl, and here was a chance to be involved in the creation of a state from the beginning. During the convention, she frequently invited delegates to her home, where she joined right in on the debates and freely offered her opinions on the most important political issues. People often said that she had the most well-thought-out opinions on the situation in Washington, probably a benefit of all of the time she spent at her father's side.

The business of the convention was to form a state constitution and to elect officials to represent the new state in Washington. The biggest issue to be decided was whether slavery should be allowed in the state, and there were strong opinions on both sides. Jessie abhorred slavery and spoke sharply to a proslavery delegate who tried to convince her that with slave labor working in her mines she could be a very wealthy woman. She said, "Surely we should keep the spirit of liberty in this land that which now breathes that spirit."

Jessie went on to exclaim that the Bentons had freed their slaves long ago and that she had often gone without a servant in California because she refused to buy slaves when they were offered to her. When one antislavery delegate heard her, he gathered others to hear her opinions. She must have been convincing, because one man said, "All the women here are crying to have servants—but if you, a Virginia lady, can get along without, they shan't have them—we'll keep clear of slave labor."

Jessie was thrilled at the news, but more excitement was yet to come. Delegates had to be elected to carry the new constitution to Washington, D.C., and John Charles was among those elected. He would be one of the senators from the territory of California. Soon, Jessie and her family would be making the trip east. It was a way to make up for the earlier court-martial, and Jessie relished the thought of seeing her father and family again.

John Charles was elected to a two-year term in the Senate, and when it ended he was ready to hurry back to the gold-mining operation in California. Jessie, even though she was pregnant, went back with him. This time, they settled in San Francisco, and there Jessie delivered a healthy son, John Charles, who they called Charley. San Francisco was a wonderful home, and with their riches the Frémonts were able to travel to Europe and to the East to see her parents several times. To the Frémonts' great joy, another son, Frank Preston, was born in 1854, but shortly thereafter, Jessie's mother died and her father lost his reelection campaign. Then another tragedy occurred: The beautiful brick mansion that Jessie loved so well in Washington burned, with her father's books and beautiful furnishings inside.

In 1855, while in Washington on a visit, the Frémonts made the decision to stay in Washington so that John Charles could run for the Republican nomination for president of the United States. Both John Charles and Jessie believed that it was the best way for both of them to take a stand against slavery, an issue that grew bigger every year. John Charles won the nomination easily, but Democrat James Buchanan won the election, and Jessie and John Charles returned at last to their California home. This time, they would live at the ranch and gold mine, the Mariposas.

Life at the Mariposas was wonderful. Jessie arranged to have several small log buildings moved together and then connected by a long veranda to serve as their house. The entire structure was white-washed, and it became known locally as the White House, partially as a nod to John Charles's political aspirations. Inside, Jessie placed the finest furnishings to be found in California at the time. French wallpaper, fine carpets, and beautiful silk draperies filled the make-shift house. She even had a piano delivered from San Francisco.

Jessie's life on the ranch with Lily, her two young sons, and John Charles might have reminded her of happy summers spent in St. Louis and at her mother's family plantation in Virginia, with outdoor living and happy family times. It wasn't always peaceful, though.

One day a messenger arrived at the house on horseback with a note that said unless Jessie abandoned her home within twenty-four hours, it would be burned and her husband would be killed. Jessie had known trouble was coming. Chief Justice Terry of the California Supreme Court had recently ruled that any mine that was left unattended, even temporarily, was free for the taking. A group of men who wanted mines of their own had decided to take advantage of the law. They organized a league called the Hornitos to drive out the mine owners and their workers and take their claims for themselves.

The Hornitos bribed the workers at one of Frémont's mines and convinced them to leave, then claimed the mine for themselves. A few of them stayed behind and the rest moved on to an adjacent mine, the Josephine. When the Hornitos arrived at the Josephine, they set up camp but could not be in legal possession of the mine because there were still a few of the workers busy deep inside. The Hornitos planned to keep supplies from reaching the miners; after starving them out, the mine would be theirs.

Even before the messenger arrived at her door, Jessie knew that somehow word had to get to the governor at Sacramento so that he would send help. John Charles was away trying to defend his mines, and Lily wanted to carry the message to a friendly mining camp, but Jessie wouldn't allow it. It was decided that seventeen-year-old Douglass Fox, called Foxy, a boy who was staying with the family, would go.

Jessie, Lily, and Foxy carefully wrapped the feet of the horse with rags to muffle the sound of its hooves, and then he set out for a friendly camp that could spare someone to send to Sacramento for help. Just after the messenger bearing the news that they must leave or be burned out left, Foxy came riding up. He had carried the message to someone who would reach the governor with the tale of their plight.

Jessie then went to Bates Tavern in Bear Valley, the headquarters of the Hornitos. Though she was frightened, she marched in and said, "What they demand is against the law. You may come and kill us—we are but women and children, and it will be easy—but you cannot kill the law."

She continued, "If the house is burned, we will camp on the land. If the men kill the colonel, we will sell the property to a corporation which will be much harder to deal with than he is." She then told the Hornitos about Foxy's ride and the message that was to be delivered to the governor and left with a flourish.

Late in the night Jessie and her family were awakened by the sounds of tin-can bombs exploding outside the house. Though frightened, they still refused to leave. They made it through the twenty-four hours unharmed. Several days later, the Hornitos' siege on the Josephine was broken when the miners convinced them that they would never leave the land and that the governor would back them up.

When they weren't fending off claim jumpers, Jessie and her family split their time in California between Mariposas and San Francisco, and as the 1850s were ending they heard more and more that war was about to break out between the North and the South. In 1861, the worst finally happened when the Confederate Army of the South fired upon Fort Sumter, starting the Civil War. John Charles was called back into active service for the Union in spite of his earlier discharge and court-martial, and the family traveled east once again to live during the war. When the war ended, Jessie and John Charles stayed in New York, as their large home in San Francisco had been appropriated by the Army for its own use and leveled when it was no longer needed. Jessie was heartbroken that they could not return to their home in the West. In her new home, she kept a painting of the Golden Gate at sunset by Bierstadt above her mantle saying, "If I should never enter that gate again, this will keep me from grieving too much. I must never part with it."

Times were good for the Frémonts in New York. They were free to travel to see family in the East and, though they missed California, John Charles and Jessie were making a life for themselves. The ever-active John Charles planned to found a railroad, and he traveled all over the East and to Europe to raise money for his plans. However, when the railroad failed in 1873 and John Charles was blamed for the failure, they had to sell their beautiful New York home and all of its contents, including the picture of the Golden Gate.

Jessie was devastated, but she, once again, already had a plan to make the money they needed to keep them on their feet. After they settled in a house in New York City, she went to see an editor at the *New York Ledger* about writing stories about her exciting life. He offered to buy all that she could provide, and she made a nice living writing for the *Ledger*, *Harper's*, and *Wide Awake*. She was constantly busy.

Soon, she had a chance to be busy in another arena. John Charles was made governor of the new Arizona Territory, and they moved to Yuma for a time, but the altitude and climate made Jessie ill, and she was forced to return to New York City alone, where she continued her writing career. After five years as governor, John Charles resigned, and Jessie thought that at last, at the ages of more than sixty and more than seventy, they could be together. John Charles moved back to New York, and both settled into a life of writing books. When John Charles grew ill in the cold climate, the couple moved to Los Angeles, with Lily as their companion.

There, Jessie, Lily, and John Charles lived until he became ill while traveling to the East to see Charley. On July 13, 1890, Jessie's dashing young officer died at his son's home in Washington, D.C.

Jessie didn't return east for the funeral; she remained in Los Angeles and asked only that her last telegram and a tiny portrait of herself be buried with John Charles. She then embarked on a number of projects that helped keep him alive in her heart, including efforts to have him cleared of his court-martial and have his name cleared from the railroad scandal.

Eventually, Jessie returned to her own affairs, settling in a Los Angeles house that the women of the city purchased for her. She continued to write, and on December 27, 1902, she died in her home with Lily beside her. She had requested to be cremated, and her ashes were sent to New York to be buried alongside John Charles. Part of her, however, will always remain in California in the legacy of a woman who had strong opinions, made stronger decisions, spoke her mind, and had a great love for her adopted state. ⚜

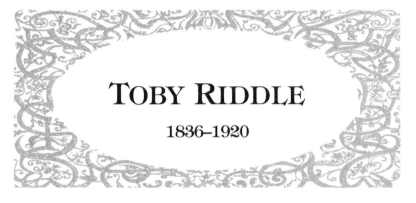

TOBY RIDDLE

1836–1920

A Strong-hearted Woman

*T*he blustering Irishman, Pat McManus, charged angrily toward Toby Riddle carrying his usual weapons, a Colt revolver and a Henry rifle, demanding to know where his horse was. Toby angrily replied, "I turned that horse loose, for the sake of your wife."

McManus was a sutler, a man who followed Army camps to peddle goods, but since the beginning of the struggle between the U.S. Army and the Modoc Indians in January 1873, he had been volunteering frequently to go into battle. Toby Riddle was a Modoc, but she was also the wife of one of the white settlers in the area. In the days before April 26, 1873, she told McManus and the other soldiers that she had had a premonition that the Modoc would attack fiercely and that the casualties would be great if they marched that day. Thinking of McManus's wife in Yreka, she frightened his horse away to keep him in the camp when her warnings seemed to fail. It wasn't the first time her warnings had gone unheeded, but this time she'd do something about it.

When Toby was born in 1836 in the part of northern California that her people called home, the Modoc occupied about two to three thousand square miles of land near the California–Oregon

Toby Riddle

border. They held beautiful Tule Lake and its eastern shore sacred. They had views of the Cascades and of the striking peak of Mount Shasta. In the southern part of their territory were forty square miles of lava beds—a maze of caverns and fissures—formed by a volcanic explosion seven thousand years ago. It was a sacred and abundant land for the Modoc, who relied on it and revered it.

At about the time that Toby was born, the United States government began a policy of forcing tribes such as the Modoc to leave their homelands and move onto reservations, which were usually on barren pieces of land that white settlers weren't interested in. The Modoc lands were remote enough that, at first, the policy didn't affect them, but in the 1840s that all began to change.

The land that the Modoc loved was also prime real estate for the white settlers who had begun to hear of the beauty and fertile lands in the Oregon Territory and realized that more bounty was to be had just to the south. Starting in the 1840s, more and more of these white settlers began moving into the Modoc homeland and claiming pieces of it for themselves.

The Modoc retaliated against this encroachment by attacking wagon trains and killing some of the newcomers, but the diseases brought by the white settlers did far more damage to the native population than the warring ways of the Modoc did to the whites. By 1848 there were only about nine hundred members of the once thriving tribe of two thousand left in their homeland.

The year 1848 was significant for another important reason that would also mark the start of even more difficulty for the Modoc. Gold was discovered in a river near the California–Oregon border, and, as a result, miners and settlers flooded into the area, founding towns and trying to get the government to force the Modoc onto reservations. These settlers made frequent complaints about the Modoc, claiming they stole cattle and raided wagon trains. In part the complaints were true, but another tribe to the north, the Klamath, were frequently responsible for depredations blamed on the Modoc. The Modoc and the Klamath were being forced into these means of survival because their native land was being overtaken by their accusers.

Into this world of change and turmoil was born a remarkable little girl who would come to be known as Toby. From early on, Toby was notorious among the Modoc people for her bravery. As a small child she was called, "The Strange Child" and "The Little Woman Chief." She was unafraid of the sacred places that most Modoc avoided and exhibited extraordinary courage as a little girl and young woman. When she was fourteen, she even helped her tribe ward off attack from a neighboring tribe alongside the boys her age who were in training as warriors. She was intelligent and, combined with her other traits, not terribly feminine by Modoc standards, though the men of her tribe thought her very attractive.

Frank Riddle, a white miner and hunter who lived in the area around the traditional Modoc territory, must also have seen how attractive the young woman was. When she was still in her teens, the two were married in spite of her family's plans for her to be married to a Modoc man. Naturally, her family was very upset that she had chosen to marry one of the people that were threatening their very existence in the land that they loved. Still, the two remained close to the Modocs, who grew to trust Frank. Toby became utterly and completely devoted to her husband.

In spite of the hardships that started in the 1840s, the Modoc managed to remain strong and independent as a tribe, if diminished in size, until the difficult winter of 1861–1862. Toby and Frank Riddle spent time with her family and knew of the Modoc's hardships, and they frequently tried to act on the Modoc's behalf with the whites in the area. Still, the cold, harsh weather killed many of the plants that the Modoc and the game animals they depended on needed for survival. Some of the tribe's elders began to suggest that they sign a treaty with the U. S. government in order to get aid for their people. It would mean moving onto a reservation and leaving their traditional homeland, but it seemed to some that they had no choice.

One of the young men, Kientpoos, who was nicknamed Captain Jack because he resembled a Yreka man named Jack, voiced his opposition to the plan, and he was joined by many others who didn't want to be moved to reservations and forced to become farmers. Still, on February 14, 1864, Chief Schonchin, representing all of the Modoc, went to see a man named Elisha Steele, who Schonchin thought was still the Indian Agent for the area. Though Steele had been removed from that post, he was still interested in brokering a peace with the Modoc, so he proceeded to negotiate. He never told Chief Schonchin that he had no authority, and the two of them agreed that the Modoc would live on their own reservation on the west side of their beloved Tule Lake. In exchange, the Modoc would allow non-Indians to pass through their territory, and they would only visit towns of whites after receiving a pass from the soldiers at Fort Klamath.

This arrangement was opposed by the white settlers who wanted the land for themselves, and no sooner had Schonchin and Steele agreed to it than it was changed by a treaty called the Council Grove Treaty that Schonchin felt compelled to sign because of the Modoc's hardship. The treaty would put Paiutes, Klamaths, and Modocs together on the same reservation in an area that had traditionally been Klamath land, and the effect would be disastrous.

Though the Klamath and the Modoc were related tribes, they always held separate territories, and the difficulties with white settlers since the beginning of the influx into their traditional homelands had created a deeper rift between the two groups. While the Modocs lived in the Klamath territory, the Klamath never hesitated to goad them about the fact that they no longer had land of their own. In addition, when the Klamath discovered that the soldiers who were present on the reservation were willing to let them go their own way without interfering, the Klamath stole lumber and fish from the Modoc and attacked Modoc women who were gathering seeds and grasses.

Captain Jack went to the Indian Agent who oversaw the reservation to ask for help, but was told never to return with a complaint again. Instead of allowing the torment to continue, Jack led a group of Modoc south, back to their homeland around Tule Lake in California. Toby and Frank, who had remained in northern California, must have been pleased to see her people return, but also must have known that more trouble was yet to come.

In the time since Captain Jack and his Modoc followers had been absent from the area, more white settlers had started ranches and farms, but there was still relative peace between the whites and the Modoc after their return. General Edward Canby, who was the commander in charge of Army operations in the Northwest, seemed inclined to let the status quo continue and even reported to Washington that, though there were difficulties between whites and Modocs, most accounts were exaggerated. Indian Superintendent Alfred Meacham tended to agree, and urged Canby to let the Indians settle the difficulties between themselves and to turn away from minor infractions of the Modoc against the whites.

Still, as emigration by whites into Modoc territory continued, many of Jack's followers began to urge that war be brought against the whites to regain traditional Modoc territory. Jack was reluctant because Alfred Meacham was trying to work with Jack to set up a separate Modoc reservation on the east side of Tule Lake around Lost River, in order to keep peace. The conditions Meacham set were simple: just don't bother the white settlers. Jack was willing to agree, but land-hungry whites wouldn't allow the land to be set aside for Indian use. Finally, in 1872, the Bureau of Indian Affairs insisted that Captain Jack and his followers be removed from the area and returned to the Klamath Reservation in Oregon. Canby and Meacham were both dismayed at the decision, but had no choice but to follow the order. For months they tried to persuade Captain Jack to leave peacefully, but Jack, supported by an even more determined group of Modoc men, refused to cooperate.

Although Jack also had no desire to go to war against the whites, many of the men under him were urging the start of a war. Jack was able to prevent his warriors from killing the whites who were coming to talk peacefully with them, but he wasn't able to keep them from making their threats. Finally, on November 28, 1872, Captain James Jackson and thirty-six men left Fort Klamath in freezing rain to find Jack and arrest him, thinking that if they were carrying enough firepower, they could get the rest of the Modoc to move peacefully to the reservation. Early in the morning on November 29, the shooting started at the village when the Modoc men refused to surrender their weapons. War was now imminent.

After the altercation at the Lost River village, Captain Jack led the warriors, women, and children who had been there to the southwest, where they would fortress themselves in the crevasses and caves of the lava beds. There they were able to barricade themselves in a deep cave that the Army couldn't find. General Canby hadn't known about the plans to force the Modoc from Lost River and would have opposed them if he did, but since blood had been shed on both sides, he had no choice but to take troops to the lava beds in order to capture Jack and end the struggle.

When Canby's troops arrived at the lava beds, Jack was still inclined to surrender, but the warriors who wanted to fight back outnumbered him. Early in the morning of January 17, 1873, the soldiers marched on the lava beds, which were shrouded by a thick fog. They were no match for the Modoc warriors who knew the secrets of the maze under their feet and were heavily armed. Thirty-seven white soldiers and volunteers were killed or wounded by the end of the day, but the Modoc were unharmed. The lava beds were a natural fortification unlike any other ever built, and Canby knew that his men were virtually powerless against it. He turned to the gentle and intelligent Toby, trusted by the Modoc and by the whites, to help him find a way out of the maze of politics and warfare he suddenly found himself in.

Toby and Frank and their son, Jeff, were allowed to come and go from the hideout in the lava beds and frequently acted as interpreters during the meetings with Canby and a group of men, including Alfred Meacham, to help work out a solution. The negotiations went on for months with the Riddles' help, though Jack was unwilling to give up anything on his side, and Canby was unable to because of his orders to remove the Modoc from their homeland. Though Canby was sympathetic to the Modoc plight and wanted to avoid further bloodshed without forcing surrender, he was powerless to do so and could barely get Jack to agree to talks.

On April 2, Toby and Frank joined the peace commissioners—as Canby, Meacham, and other men from the Army and surrounding area were termed—as interpreters in a face-to-face meeting with Captain Jack. Jack demanded a reservation on the Lost River, removal of the soldiers, and no trials for the Modocs who had killed soldiers and civilians in the battle at the lava beds. Because of his orders from the government, Canby couldn't agree, so the meeting was a failure. Still, both sides agreed to erect a tent halfway between the soldiers' camp and the fortification at the lava beds, where they could continue to negotiate a settlement.

On April 5, during a meeting at the tent, Toby passed Jack's final offer on to Canby. Jack said he was willing to accept the lava beds, where they had held off the Army for so long, as a substitute reservation. Without the authority from Washington, D.C., Canby could not promise anything, and it seemed to him that Jack's offer was not truly a serious one. Still, the commissioners accepted an offer to meet with the Modoc at the tent on April 10 to talk over a possible peace agreement that involved the lava beds as a settlement.

Toby was becoming increasingly worried that the standoff would not end without serious bloodshed, and during a visit to the lava beds on April 9, a man named Weium followed her and her son out of the rocks and confirmed her fears. He said, "Toby, tell Old Man Meacham and all them men not to come to the council tent again. They all get killed."

As Toby and Jeff returned to the camp, she was very afraid for the whites and also for herself, because she would have to go along to the tent with the commissioners as an interpreter. She said to Jeff, who was just a small boy, "My son, in case I and your father get killed, stay with Mr. Fairchild. . . . But if I can help it, the Peace Commissioners shall not meet Captain Jack and his men in council any more."

Jeff later remembered that his mother sobbed as if her heart would break, as she tried to think of what to do. He was unable to control himself when Alfred Meacham greeted them at the camp with a jovial question about their dealings with Captain Jack. The small boy blurted out the whole story of the meeting with Weium.

Meacham was alarmed enough that he called together the other commissioners to hear Toby out. She addressed them: "I must ask you, before I tell you, not to tell any of the Modocs where you was told what I am going to tell you men, and by whom. My life and man's life and little boy's life will be in great danger. . . ."

All of the men swore that they would not reveal her secret, and she poured out to them the tale of Weium's warning. "The next time you meet Jack and his men in council, you will all be shot to death. What I tell you is the truth. Take my warning. Do not meet the people in council any more. If you do, you will be carried to this camp, dead."

In spite of Toby's warning and her obvious fear, Canby dismissed her words because he was sure the Modoc would not attack with such a large force of soldiers nearby. Meacham and two of the other commissioners wanted to at least delay the meeting, and they told Toby that they would postpone it if at all possible. Another of the commissioners, a man named Thomas, agreed with Canby, and when two of the Modocs, Bogus and Boston, rode into the Army camp the next day, April 10, he asked them, "Why do you Indians want to kill us?"

Bogus and Boston assured Thomas over and over that was not the case, and asked who told him that. Without thinking of his promise to protect her, Thomas immediately revealed that Toby was the informant. Both Bogus and Boston doubled their reassurances, and Boston ran to Jack to tell him of the leak, while Bogus remained in camp to meet with Meacham and give further promises that the commissioners were not to be harmed.

Soon a runner came into the Army camp from the lava beds to say that the meeting was postponed until the next day, April 11, and that Captain Jack wished to see Toby at once. As she bravely mounted her horse, Meacham tried to stop her from returning to the lava beds, but she said, "I am not afraid to go, Meacham." Still, she accepted his gun to carry with her.

Meacham later recalled:

> She parted with her little boy, ten years old, several times before she succeeded in mounting her horse. Clasping him to her breast, she would set him down and start, and then run to him and catch him up again, each time seeming more affected to the last, until, at last, her courage was high enough and, saying a few words in a low voice to her husband, she rode off.

Once at the stronghold in the lava beds, Toby stood in front of Captain Jack, who demanded to know where she had gotten her information. At first, Toby wove a fanciful tale of the spirits coming to her in a dream to warn her of the danger. Jack wouldn't accept the lie, and finally Toby blurted out the truth about her informer. She said, "I didn't dream it. The spirits did not tell me. One of your men told me. I won't tell you who it was. Shoot me, if you dare. But there are soldiers there. You touch me and they will fire on you and not a Modoc will escape."

After her speech, she drew Meacham's gun against the rifles of most of the Modoc men, while they demanded her death. Jack and eight men went to protect her, and knocked the rifles aside. He insisted to Toby that her informer had been wrong, that he meant to kill no one the next day, and sent her back to camp with an escort.

When Toby returned with the protection of the eight men who had come to her aid in the stronghold, her husband and son rejoiced, as did the rest of the camp. She reported the events of the meeting, but would not shake her belief that the commissioners were in danger if they went to the meeting the next day, nor would she stop her warnings.

On the night of April 10, Canby wrote to his wife, "Don't be discouraged or gloomy, darling. I will take good care of myself and come home as soon as possible." The next morning, Toby urged him again not to go to the tent, and he laughed and said to some of his men, "Well, brother officers, I bid you all a last farewell. From what Riddle says, this is my last day."

Canby and the commissioners, along with Toby and Frank, headed off to the tent in the mid-morning. When they arrived they could see clearly that the Modoc men were not unarmed as had been agreed, but at first, the meeting seemed to go as planned. Then, with neither side willing to budge, at one o'clock in the afternoon, Jack shouted, *"Ot-we kantux-e"* ("all ready") and he, along with the other warriors who were with them, opened fire at the group of commissioners. The mostly unarmed group was helpless, and except for the

Riddles, who were under Jack's protection, only two were able to escape, one by running toward the soldiers' camp, and the other, Alfred
Meacham, when Toby shouted "The soldiers are coming!" and frightened away the Modoc warrior who was trying to scalp him.

The killing of the peace commissioners was the end for Captain Jack and his men, as the Army redoubled its efforts to force
them out of the lava beds and into surrender. Several other battles
would ensue, including the one on April 26, when Toby frightened
away Pat McManus' horse knowing the Modoc were leading the
soldiers into a trap; she was thinking of his wife, and perhaps of
Canby's wife as well, since she had been unable to prevent his death.

Eventually, the Modoc were forced to surrender, and Captain
Jack was put on trial, along with a number of other Modoc. Toby
served as an interpreter along with Frank, and both were devastated
when Jack refused to testify and was eventually found guilty and
sentenced to hang. Jack was furious because the men who had forced
him to attack that day at the tent were going free, because they had
agreed to capture him and testify against him.

Up until the night before the fateful meeting with the commissioners at the tent, Jack had remained opposed to any killing,
though he was fairly certain that he would no longer be able to
restrain the men under him. He had been outvoted by the other
Modoc and forced to attack that April day.

In 1874, Toby, Frank, and Jeff went on a lecture tour in the
East with Alfred Meacham, who had recovered from his near scalp-
ing. Meacham's motive was the money he could make from lectures
about the highly publicized Modoc Indian war. Perhaps Toby was
motivated by the thought that she could somehow vindicate her
people by sharing the truth about their plight. She continued that
desire when, in 1914, she helped Jeff write *The History of the Modoc War.*

It was possible, even probable, that Toby—or Winema, as
Meacham had called her on the lecture circuit—knew more about

the Modoc Indian War than anyone living and had more reason to be distressed by the events than anyone else. During the time that Captain Jack and his band were holed up in the lava beds, she, Frank, and Jeff were the only people allowed to come and go, and the only ones who knew their way in and out.

Mere premonitions had not caused Toby to warn Canby before he headed to the tent on that fateful day, nor had they fueled her need to drive McManus' horse away. While she had been in the caves and slots underground, Weium had followed her out of the lava beds because he knew with certainty what was going to happen on April 11. It is likely that before the battle on April 26, where the Army was ambushed and suffered severe casualties, someone else had come to her to warn her of the danger and she had claimed to learn of it in a dream.

Whether or not Captain Jack, who had been so opposed to the escalation of violence and protected her when she came to the lava beds that night, had given permission to Weium to tell Toby of the planned surprise attack, no one will ever know. It is a secret that died with Toby in 1920 at the Klamath Reservation.

During the Modoc war, the Denver, Colorado, *Tribune*, reported that little boys in the city, hearing of the battles from their parents, were playing Modoc Indians in their backyards. Presumably, little girls weren't invited to participate, since to the outside world it appeared that no women were involved in the war—no one had ever heard of Toby Riddle. Still, with the lecture tour that followed, and in the years to come when the story of the Modoc war was recorded, she would not be forgotten. In Oregon, the Winema National Forest is named for the brave woman who was trusted by all and tried to keep the peace. Roughly translated, *Winema* means stronghearted woman, and Toby Riddle was certainly that. ❧

SARAH WINCHESTER
1840–1922

Woman of Mystery

*A*t around five o'clock on the morning of April 18, 1906, sections of earth stretching throughout California and Oregon were set shaking by a fierce earthquake that toppled buildings, set fires blazing, and essentially razed the city of San Francisco. Just a few miles to the south in San Jose, three stories of Sarah Pardee Winchester's seven-story house lay in ruins around the remaining structure, and Sarah was nowhere to be found. Nearly half the day had gone by, and her niece, Marian Merriman, and the servants had yet to find the tiny, sixty-six-year-old woman. For hours they combed the wreckage, fearing the worst, and unable to hear the faint cries of the panicked Sarah from her second-floor bedroom. They thought she had gone to another part of the house for the night, as she frequently did.

When at last they began to pry the wreckage away from the door of the bedroom where Sarah was trapped, they feared for what they might find; but when they freed her, she was shaken but stubborn of mind. The front thirty rooms of her ninety-room mansion would have to be sealed off and never used again, she declared. The friendly spirits who directed her in building her home had told her that the earthquake was caused by the evil spirits who thought she had spent too much time working on those rooms.

For six months, Sarah Winchester lived on a luxurious barge in a bay off Redwood City while the rubble from the collapse of so much house could be cleared away and the front thirty rooms shut off for good. Then she moved back in and set her carpenters, pipefitters, foreman, and servants back to work on the project she kept them busy with for thirty-eight years: the building of what is known as the Winchester Mystery House.

Sarah Pardee was born in 1840 in New Haven, Connecticut, far from what was then the Mexican territory known as California. Her father, Leonard Pardee, was a carriage manufacturer, and he and her mother, Sarah Burns Pardee, provided the best in education and culture for their daughter, who was to become known as "the belle of New Haven."

Sarah Pardee was an extremely intelligent young woman who took advantage of all the wonders that her parents' wealth provided for her. She was educated at fine private schools and spoke as many as four languages fluently, including Turkish. She also played the piano beautifully and was considered all that an accomplished and bright Victorian woman should be.

In 1862, she made a fortuitous match of which her parents could be proud, when she married William Wirt Winchester and prepared for life as a prominent matron in New England society. William was the son of Oliver Fisher Winchester, the lieutenant governor of Connecticut who was better known as the manufacturer of the infamous and extremely popular Winchester Repeating Rifle. Sarah and William's life together was very happy, until the mysterious death in 1866 of their infant daughter, Annie, from marasmus, a disorder that makes it impossible for the body to absorb nutrients from food.

WINCHESTER MYSTERY HOUSE. SAN JOSE, CALIFORNIA

Sarah Winchester
Taken by a gardener hiding in some bushes, this is the only photo-
graph of Sarah Winchester at her Mystery House known to be in
existence today.

Sarah slumped into a deep depression from which she never fully recovered, though her love for her husband must have helped her cope with her grief. The couple was never to have another child, and fifteen years later, William died from tuberculosis, leaving Sarah utterly alone and completely devastated.

Despondent over the death of her beloved husband, Sarah was at a loss physically and emotionally when she made the decision to leave her comfortable New England home to go west to the then booming state of California. Some say that her friends and relatives recommended that she move west for her health. Others say that she felt strangely compelled to consult with a psychic about the deaths of her husband and child as she searched for an explanation for her grief, and that the psychic had directed her to go west.

Sarah's interest in the occult and in seeking spiritual advice from mediums and psychics was not unusual for a well-to-do Victorian woman. Many people of that era were fascinated with contacting spirits in order to seek answers to questions about an afterlife, to contact long-dead friends and relatives, or just to be entertained for an evening by a psychic who would come to their homes to hold a séance. It is unlikely, however, that many people were as changed by their visits with psychics as Sarah Winchester.

The medium Sarah visited in Boston told her that spirits were haunting her family. To be specific, she was told that the souls of people killed by the Winchester Repeating Rifle—now known throughout the world as "the gun that won the West" for its role in opening up the Western frontier to settlers—were out for vengeance against her. Her daughter and husband had died untimely deaths because of their association with the rifle, and she might be next!

However, the medium said there was one way that Sarah might avoid the same fate. Sarah was instructed to move to the West and to find an unfinished house that she could add onto in order to build a great house for the spirits to inhabit. As long as the construction on the house never ceased, she might be spared and the spirits might be appeased.

By this time, Sarah Winchester was a wealthy woman with no ties to keep her in the East, so at the age of forty-four she went to visit a niece in Menlo Park, California, and while she was there discovered the place where she would build her great mansion. In 1884, she purchased an eight-room farmhouse just west of San Jose in the Santa Clara Valley, hired carpenters to work in shifts around the clock, and set to work creating new plans for her house and revising them over and over again while her staff tried to satisfy her whims. By 1900, the eight-room farmhouse had become the seven-story mansion that would topple when the earthquake struck in 1906.

Sarah Winchester's fortune was undoubtedly a matter of some speculation to her Santa Clara Valley neighbors. In reality, she was rich beyond almost anyone's wildest dreams. Upon her husband's death, she had received several million dollars in cash and 777 shares of stock in the highly successful Winchester Repeating Arms factory. When her mother-in-law died in 1897, she received two thousand more shares, giving her just under fifty percent of the company's stock. Unbelievably wealthy before the death of her husband's mother, the increase in her holdings meant that she had an average income of one thousand dollars a day.

With her wealth, she would purchase building materials of mahogany and redwood, custom-designed stained-glass windows, and roll upon roll of embossed wallpaper imported from England. She also paid her staff of round-the-clock carpenters a small fortune—three dollars a day in a time when the average wage was half that amount. She expected them to work for it, however, sometimes coming to them with new plans for additions in the middle of the night or interrupting their work in one area to make them start on another. Her demands were unrelenting and probably extremely frustrating.

Sarah designed the house herself, and the story goes that she made its hallways and passages as confusing as possible to fool the evil spirits that might be lurking all around her at any moment. An architect designed only one room in the house, the grand ballroom. It is a masterpiece of exquisite wood paneling and a parquet floor made of mahogany, teak, maple, rosewood, oak, and white ash. Not a single nail was used in its construction. The entire room cost the enormous sum of nine thousand dollars in a time when a very comfortable house could be constructed for about a thousand dollars.

Sarah's odd notions made their way into that beautiful room, as well. She was superstitious to an extreme because of her relationship with the spirit world, and she made use of the number thirteen as a good luck talisman throughout the house. When the imported silver chandelier from Germany held only twelve candles, she had it specially altered to fit thirteen in it before hanging it at the central point of the thirteen panels of ceiling. Two beautiful stained-glass windows flank the fireplace, which remained unfinished after the 1906 earthquake. One bears the phrase, "Wide unclasp the tables of their thoughts," and the other reads, "These same thoughts people this little world." No one knows what significance these words from Shakespeare's *Troilus and Cressida* and *Richard II*, respectively, had for her.

Some of the ingenious innovations in her home and in the inventions that eased the lives of her servants were Sarah's ideas. In one of her conservatories, she had a zinc subfloor installed that slanted toward the outer wall of the house. When it came time to water the houseplants, the wood panels of the upper floor were removed, the plants were moved into the conservatory, and the excess water would drain out of the house into the gardens outside. The floor was zinc so it would not rust.

Sarah also had brass corner plates installed on her staircases to keep dust from accumulating in the corners, saving work for the house servants. In addition, she invented and tried to patent a sink with a built-in washboard and soap dish, to make the efforts of washing clothes and linens less trying. She installed elevators and other modern conveniences. For her own convenience, she had call buttons for the servants installed that let them know who she wanted and where she was in the enormous house. The thirteen carpenters, ten housekeepers, eight gardeners, and two chauffeurs were expected to be on call twenty-four hours a day.

In spite of the high rate of pay and the labor-saving devices she had installed, she must have made life truly miserable for many who worked for her. Her eccentricities led to strange features in the house that allowed her to spy on her servants and workmen at all times, including windows in almost every door and into every room in the house, even bathrooms. In her south conservatory, she placed 250 windows—in the walls, the ceiling, and even the floor—so she could watch the servants working below.

She was always making new plans for the house, usually at 2 o'clock in the morning in the special séance room she had designed. There was only one door into the room, but there were three separate exits that—in theory—only Sarah and her spirit friends knew about. One was the door you entered by; another, next to it, was a door that opened into an empty space with a drop to the kitchen sink below. There was also a secret passageway through a cupboard into the room behind the séance room, where if you shut the door behind you, you were stuck. In the cupboard there were thirteen separate coat hooks, perhaps for thirteen midnight visitors.

Among the strange requests that the spirits were supposed to have dreamed up were that a workman paint an entire room with red enamel and asked to repaint it in white the next day. A room was also built, now called the Hall of Fires, with seven different sources of heat. There were three forced-hot-air registers and four fireplaces. She also had what was probably a gorgeous fifteen-hundred-dollar Tiffany stained glass window installed. It was the most expensive window in the house, but no light would ever shine through it, giving it the sparkle it was designed for, because on the other side of the window was the wall to another room. In her guest reception room, an odd choice for a room since she received almost no guests, pieces of the fireplace were installed upside down at her request. Posts throughout the house and the outside porches were installed the same way. The floor in the magnificent reception room, a beautiful parquet, required the work of one man for a solid year.

Sarah and her niece Marian enjoyed a luxurious life in the mansion with its construction all around them. They were served excellent wines with the very fine dinners prepared by the housekeepers and after-dinner drinks from the well-stocked mansion wine cellar—until Sarah went to make a selection one day and found an ominous-looking black handprint on the wall. A workman probably made it inadvertently, but Sarah took it as a sign from the spirits that she was to abandon drinking all alcohol, and she had the cellar walled up.

It was curious that Sarah allowed few guests in her fabulous mansion. When Teddy Roosevelt wanted to visit, he was offered the carriage house door rather than the front doors, which only Sarah used. He chose not to make an entrance after all and headed on his way. Her niece was constantly with her, and they frequently visited other family members in their comfortable San Jose homes, also provided by the Winchester fortune.

The servants were never allowed to see Sarah's face, as she nearly always wore a veil, and she would allow no pictures to be taken of her. Only her spirit friends, the spirits that guided her through the building of her magnificent, mysterious home, had full access to her. She let them come and go through the forty-seven fireplaces that were scattered throughout the house for their convenience, since she believed that the spirits liked to move through the chimneys.

Sarah didn't spend all of her wealth on the house. She also endowed charitable institutions and supported her family in their endeavors. She even bought a luxury yacht, and though she never used it, perhaps the spirits enjoyed midnight sails. As she aged, her requests for the homebuilders became ever stranger, although many of her ideas were logical and intelligent. The many staircases in the house were replaced with even more switch-backing low risers that helped her move up and down through the house, because her arthritis crippled her so that she could only lift her feet about two inches from the ground. She also had a specially designed shower put into her bathroom (which had thirteen windows in a spider web design that she favored) with a spray that surrounded her at an angle calculated for her tiny four foot, ten inch frame. The shower was thermostatically controlled and very modern.

Even though she had survived the 1906 earthquake and had managed to appease the spirits by following their direction for so many years, Sarah must have known that even if the building of the house continued forever, she would eventually succumb to old age. When she quietly passed away in her sleep at the age of 82 in 1922, the house was shut down, the furniture moved out over a period of two months, and the goods were sold at auction. Half-finished rooms remained throughout the house, and materials for more rooms still stood in her storerooms.

Now, visitors come in droves to see the mystery and complete the mile-long tour through the 26,000-square-foot mansion, seeing most of the 160 rooms and their contents. One room they never see is the wine cellar, which has never been found. Most of the rooms are empty, but some of them have been furnished in the period. Perhaps they are not really empty though; perhaps Mrs. Winchester's spirit has joined her spirit friends, now delightedly watching the awe and amazement on visitors' faces. Even if the building of the Winchester Mystery House was really guided by a lonely woman's need for a hobby, rather than by the spirit world, it might comfort her to know that she has attained eternal life to a certain extent in the legacy left for generations of visitors. ✤

FLORENCE HUTCHINGS
1864–1881

Zanita of Yosemite

The passengers in the stagecoach craned their necks to peer out of the tiny windows and gazed at the wonder that surrounded them as they were jolted along the steep, rutted road into their destination valley. Around them were the magnificent peaks that had encouraged their visit to the wonderland of rocks, waterfalls, and trees of the Yosemite Valley.

Before their eyes had received their fill of the glorious sights around them, a strange figure in a costume that seemed to come out of a quaint tale appeared. Poised on horseback and grasping at a scarlet bridle was a slight personage in tall boots, a wide-brimmed hat, and a flowing cape. At the sight of the stage, the horse reared up and Florence Hutchings removed the hat with a flourish. "Welcome, welcome!" she cried.

The sixteen-year-old girl in trousers and on horseback—sitting astride and not on a demure sidesaddle—was a shocking sight to most of the passengers she greeted as they entered the valley she called home. Most had no idea she wasn't a boy until her voice cried out her gleeful tidings. During the days of their visit, however, they would come to know the charming young girl well, for she was a

YOSEMITE RESEARCH LIBRARY

Florence Hutchings at age 6

self-appointed tour guide and interpreter for everyone who wished to experience Yosemite.

Florence Hutchings was born on August 23, 1864, at her father's hotel in the Yosemite Valley, where tourists were already flocking in droves, though it had only recently been opened up to exploration and given federal protection by President Abraham Lincoln because of its great beauty. Florence was the first white child to be born in the valley—a pioneer born to pioneers.

Florence's grandmother was Florantha Sproat, who had been born Florantha Thompson in 1811, in Middleborough, Massachusetts. Florantha's father was the distinguished portrait painter Cephas Thompson, and she grew up around books, paintings, ancient tapestries, and distinguished company. John Marshall, chief justice of the Supreme Court, was one of her father's subjects and friends. Her two brothers and one sister were also artistic, but Florantha's means of distinguishing herself would not be with a brush and palette, but ultimately through adventure and good cooking.

In 1838, she married Granville Temple Sproat and traveled with him to the Ojibway Indian Mission at La Pointe, Wisconsin, where he taught and she cooked. Eventually the two moved with their daughters to the booming state of California and to San Francisco, where Florantha made her way by running boarding houses. Sproat ceased to be a part of his wife's life after 1854, but she and her two daughters remained in San Francisco, where daughter Elvira married James Mason Hutchings, an educated man who ran a literary journal, in 1860.

After Yosemite became a tourist destination, Hutchings determined that a hotel business there would make his fortune, and he settled there with his wife and mother-in-law in 1864. Florantha was the true business partner in the enterprise, as she was the chief cook and housekeeper at the hotel, but Elvira helped as well. They were operating the hotel by April 1864, and Florence, or Floy, as she was called, was born in August of that year.

Floy flourished in the free-and-easy atmosphere of the Yosemite Valley, where she lived in the hotel, which was distinguished by having a tree growing through the kitchen. When the room had been added, Hutchings did not want to cut the 175-foot-high incense cedar down, so he built around it. Since the circumference of the trunk was 24 feet, it must have been an annoyance to the chef, Florantha Sproat, but she made do, hanging her pots from nails stuck in its trunk. It was a rough and new location for any family life, and Floy seemed to take the cue that she was not to be like other girls, but would forge a new way for herself.

She was as ungirl-like as she could be, collecting frogs and toads, mocking the birds, and learning to growl like a grizzly bear. In fact, it was her chief complaint in life that she was not born a boy, but she didn't let the mere fact of biology stop her from making her way like a boy. She scorned dolls for the chance to seesaw for hours or to tag along after the men who frequented the hotel. Eadward Muybridge, a famous photographer, delighted in teaching the toddler to say in a childish lisp, "I used to smoke a meerchaum, but now I smoke a 'torn tob'." Indeed, Muybridge was probably surprised, however, when Floy began to roll and smoke her own cigarettes at a tender age.

In 1867, Floy's life was made more complete with the birth of a sister, Gertrude, called Cosie, and in 1869 by a brother, William. William was born with a crippling condition in his back so he wasn't the playmate Floy might have hoped for, but Cosie joined in Floy's escapades without much hesitation. Both girls were superb horsewomen, and they would frequently gather horses for tourists to form a saddle train for group excursions. The men at the stables would tease Floy into riding the wildest of the horses bareback, which she stuck on with admirable tenacity.

The girls were also friends with the Native American children who lived in the valley. Cosie later remembered that she and Floy would ask their grandmother, Florantha, to make them cornbread, even though they didn't like it, because ". . . the little Indians loved it! So we swapped it to them for nutpatty—a delicious little cake make from finely ground acorns, which Florence and I ate with relish."

One of the more influential older friends in Florence's life came to the Yosemite Valley in 1868. His name was John Muir, and for a time the Scotsman worked as a sawyer in the Hutchings' sawmill at the base of Yosemite Falls. He would later become known as an ardent conservationist and author. Muir and Hutchings didn't get along, but Muir would take the girls to the barn for fresh milk from the cows, since he thought that the fad diets their mother tried to impose on them were hard on them. His love of nature inspired both Floy and Cosie, who tramped about after him as he explored the valley, giving them a chance to know their home from the bottoms of its falls to the tops of its peaks. The girls might have taken their surroundings for granted, having never known anything else, but the reverence their mentor showed for the surrounding world was evidence to them of their special childhood.

Floy's unconventional spirit and actions attracted attention—both positive and negative—from many adults who visited Yosemite, but she could also impress people with her mature conversations, and she had a great humbleness in the face of nature. On one of her frequent hikes, she recorded in the register at Snow's Hotel, near Nevada and Vernal Falls—a remote, dreamlike location: "'Beautiful,' 'Wonderful' how come you are? For what has nature caused this awe inspiring deep cañon and high towering peaks for it is to remind one there is a God, and that his works are the works of nature? that his works are wonderful beyond comprehension?"

In spite of Florence's hoydenish demeanor, it was perhaps unfair of Therese Yelverton, vicountess of Avenmore, to characterize Florence as she did in her novel, *Zanita.* Yelverton spent the summer of 1870 in Yosemite, and based her novel on the friendship between John Muir and Floy. The title character, Zanita, was based on Mrs. Yelverton's impressions of Floy, but greatly exaggerated. The physical description of the heroine could be matched point for point with a photograph of the young Floy, and for the casual observer it would be easy to see the commonality in their characters, for Zanita was a tomboy who roamed the mountains and befriended curmudgeons, but she was also a completely selfish creature who died young as a result. Selfish young Floy was not, as the many guests who benefited from her kindness could attest.

James Hutchings was evicted from his landholdings in Yosemite in about 1875 because of a political battle, when Floy had just turned eleven. The family moved to San Francisco, where the children's lives were about to be impacted in a much larger fashion than removing them from their beloved Yosemite had. Their mother, Elvira, left James Hutchings, though James and the children remained with Florantha Sproat in her San Francisco home, and Elvira only saw her children at church and on rare visits to her own home in the city. Elvira's love for Yosemite and its beauties remained with her throughout her life, but only her children would return to its glories.

James, Florantha, and the children returned to Yosemite every summer, spending the winter in the city. In 1876, James Hutchings met a young widow named Augusta Ladd Sweetland, who accompanied them to the park and camped with them during the summer of 1876. James, Florantha, Florence, and Augusta climbed many of the valley's famous peaks during their camping stay, including the formidable Half Dome. In 1879, Augusta and James were married, and in 1880, James was given the guardianship of Yosemite. He settled his small family in their old log cabin near the hotel with its kitchen tree.

Augusta might have despaired at the sight of her new stepdaughters, particularly Floy, on her horse and in trousers. If she tried to curb Floy and Cosie's wild ways, it was to no avail. Still, though Floy horrified people with her swearing, smoking, and fearless escapades, her little kindnesses were never forgotten. Though she would still say that she was sorry she was not a boy, she had developed softer tendencies by the time she was sixteen years old. Her informed tours around the valley floor and errand running were greatly appreciated by the tourists who came to view her beloved home, and local children adored her. In addition, Floy had discovered and become a convert to Christianity, and regardless of her outward appearance, she had an inward reverence for a larger power that had created the magic of the world she lived in. When the Yosemite Chapel was built in 1879, she became its caretaker and swept, dusted, decorated, and in all other ways prepared it for the few times when a preacher came into the valley to hold services— she would even ring the bell to summon her neighbors to the chapel.

Floy also had a dear friend in thirteen-year-old Effie Crippen. The Hutchings girls had always known the Crippen girls, who had also grown up in the park. The Crippens were as fearless as Floy and Cosie, and Effie's older sister, Fannie, who went so far as to sign her name "Frank" Crippen, was the wildest of the Crippen girls, rivaling even Floy's fame. Effie, though a brave young woman herself, joining the family on many hikes and climbs over the rocks to places like Nevada Falls, was a gifted and sensitive girl who recited poetry and made beautiful sketches. She lived in a dream world and slept with a volume of Longfellow's poems under her pillow. Her sweet disposition and quiet activities would have been quite a contrast to her friend Floy's escapades. Still, the two were nearly inseparable.

Tragedy struck when, in 1881, Effie was wading in Mirror Lake and she stepped on a jagged piece of glass left by someone who had consumed the contents of a wine bottle and cast the empty shell away. She severed an artery and during the three-mile horseback ride home lost a tremendous amount of blood. Over the next few days she bled slowly to death, as no doctor was available to repair her foot. Floy mourned sorrowfully for her friend.

Though Mrs. Yelverton's book based on the life of Florence Hutchings must be construed as fiction, it also turned out to be prophetic, for barely three weeks after her dear friend bled to death, Floy died suddenly and tragically at the age of seventeen. The accounts of the accident vary, but Cosie Hutchings recalled:

> . . . my sister and a party of friends were climbing the Ledge trail when someone above her accidentally loosened a large rock and it rolled down, striking Florence. She was badly injured and was carried back to the cabin. She died the following day.

Her funeral was a sober affair, held in the Big Tree Room of the hotel that had been her earliest childhood home. All remembered her friendship with Effie Crippen and recalled her climbing and scampering through the same places where tragedy had befallen them both. As a tribute to Floy Hutchings, who was an original soul in an original place, a 12,507-foot peak was named for the girl. Mount Florence stands between Mount Maclure and Mount Lyell, a fitting memorial to the girl who wanted to be a boy, but who defined the spirit of the pioneering woman in Yosemite.

MARY AUSTIN

1868–1934

A Woman of Genius

$\mathcal{N}$ine days had passed since the agonizing hours that led up to baby Ruth's birth, so Mary's mother insisted that she get out of bed. Mary did as she was told, but within a day she was flat on her back at the doctor's orders. Even the thought of the grueling labor she had been through was painful, so she could scarcely bear to think of it. She had felt so utterly alone during the labor, even in her mother's house, especially when the doctor was called away for four hours in the middle of it to amputate a man's leg. Still, the baby was beautiful, and Mary's brothers Jim and George doted on their little niece. Mary herself looked forward to a much closer relationship with her daughter than she had ever had with Susanna Hunter, her own mother. Still, it would have been nice if Wallace, her husband, had been able to come for the birth of their child. They hadn't seen each other for months, since September when Mary had left Wallace in Inyo, California, to stay with her mother and brothers in Bakersfield until the birth of her baby.

While Mary was still confined to her bed, completely debilitated from the difficulties of her labor, she received news that she and her husband were deeply in debt, and that their creditors were

Mary Austin

demanding immediate payment. Mary had known that business had not gone well for Wallace since their marriage, but she had no idea how much they owed until she received notice that she was being held liable for the debts he had incurred. Wallace had not earned more than a few dollars since the irrigation company he had been working for failed, and they were ruined. The blow to Mary, especially coming so soon after her terrifying labor, was terrible. Mary's mother and brothers urged Mary to divorce him, as their belief in staying out of debt far surpassed their abhorrence of divorce. Still, that would have made Mary totally dependent on her family, and she was too independent for the sort of life that would mean for her and for her tiny daughter, Ruth.

Mary would later write about her feelings after Ruth's birth when life was at its worst in her autobiography, *Earth Horizon.* She chose to write of herself in the third person, as if making herself into a character from one of her novels.

> She still believed in the solution of the personal problem by the application of intelligence. The surprises of the last two years had been disconcerting, and the obligations of her condition had prevented their being forcefully met. But she thought if she could only talk things over with her husband. . . . This was difficult to understand, but Mary felt confident that there was an explanation. She would go to her husband and they would talk things out and come to an understanding and begin all over again. There was nothing two intelligent people couldn't do together if they set about it.

In fact, Mary had already made headway toward just the solution that was called for when the news came of their financial ruin— long before she spoke to Wallace about it.

It had been a long road for Mary Hunter Austin from her childhood home in Carlinville, Illinois, where she was born at midnight on September 9, 1868, to her mother's house in Bakersfield, California, where her own daughter was born. Her mother was Susanna Savilla Graham Hunter, the daughter of a staunchly Methodist Carlinville family and the latest in a long line of sturdy and intelligent pioneer women. Susanna was extremely well read and intelligent, and had dreamed of a career in teaching (she did teach for one year) or in writing, but when she was nineteen she did as her family expected and married Carlinville attorney Captain George Hunter. George had immigrated to the United States from England in the late 1850s, and he had taken up the practice of law in Carlinville, where he opened an office over Susanna's father's pharmacy.

In 1861 when the Civil War broke out, George enlisted in the Union Army, and shortly thereafter he and Susanna were married. From the day of their marriage, George's life became Susanna's life. She traveled south with him during the Civil War and lived in Army camps during the first few years of their marriage, returning to Carlinville only to bear two children who died in infancy. During the war, George was constantly ill with malaria, which kept him at a desk for most of his service and kept Susanna by his side nursing him. The symptoms of the fever would plague him for the rest of his life.

After George's term of service was up in 1864, the young couple settled in Carlinville, and he resumed his law practice. In 1866 their first son, James Milo Hunter, was born. Susanna was always fearful for the family's financial situation because it was difficult for George to make a living, sick as he always was. She grew more anxious when she learned another child was on the way, and she was unable to welcome the new baby with great joy. Their first son, James, was born with a malformed leg, and she constantly fussed over him.

With a sick husband and a lame child, she was weary already.

When Mary was born, she was an unlovely child, scrawny with a perpetually downturned mouth, and, though it would be unfair to say she was unloved, she may not have been her mother's first priority. Her husband's needs and those of her son nearly always came first with her, and, as Mary grew older, her relationship with her mother did not improve. Susanna disapproved of Mary's habit of "storying," telling the stories of events as though she had been there, when it was clear she had not. She would also become exasperated when Mary, who was a very perceptive child, would blurt out embarrassing things in company that everyone was thinking, but no one would ever have said out loud. With a red face, Susanna would exclaim, "I think the child is possessed." No punishment Susanna could conceive would cure Mary of her habits, and their encounters could be very disagreeable indeed.

Mary was very close to her father, however, and she spent many happy hours with him looking at books in his study or walking with him in all seasons through the area surrounding the small farm where they lived. George spent many hours in the outdoors, as it seemed to help relieve his bouts of illness. Mary's time with her father was precious to her and helped her develop her love of nature. Walking at his side, she learned to appreciate moist spring days in the sun as much as the crisp winter tromps through snow.

The only other person Mary was very close to as a child was her younger sister, Jennie. Born when Mary was barely two, Jennie was a beautiful, sweet baby, not intractable and frown-faced like Mary. Jennie was everyone's favorite, including her older sister's. The two little girls would spend many hours together as they grew older, and, indeed, it seemed to Mary as though Jennie was one of her only friends.

There was, however, another "person" in Mary's life more important than any other. Mary had learned to read at the young age of four by studying along with her brother, Jim, who had just started school. She discovered something very important when he was learning his vowels one day, and her mother explained the letter "I" to Mary by saying when Mary pointed to her own eye, "No. I, myself, I want a drink, I-Mary." Suddenly, Mary realized that inside her was a person who didn't have to be the little girl that everyone ignored or complained about. She came to associate the printed word with a strong inner self that she called I-Mary. When she was I-Mary, she knew everything or could learn anything, and she had a secret power.

When Mary went to school at the young age of five, I-Mary spoke up when the teacher chided her for looking at a book when she should have been studying her letters. I-Mary told the teacher that she had been reading, not just looking at the book. When the teacher disputed her story, the principal intervened, and when Mary proved that she could read, she was moved two grades ahead of her age level.

Mary's reading skills were excellent. She read everything that she could get her hands on. Her math and social skills were sorely lacking, and her lack of graces compounded with the fact that she was unattractive by the standards of the day and considered strange because of her imaginative tale-spinning and her extraordinary intelligence, kept her lonely. Jennie and her father were the only people with whom she was close, and she found solace in them, in I-Mary, and in nature.

In 1877, however, events that would change Mary's life forever began. Her father's health grew worse and worse, and after his fourth child, a son, named George, was born in that year, George Hunter, Senior, died on October 29, 1878. Mary was devastated by the loss of her father, and her mother, the one person who could have endeavored to make the loss less keenly felt, was preoccupied with the baby and worries about how she was to feed her small brood of children. Jim was twelve years old, and his mother depended on him to support her. The two of them were very close indeed. Jennie and

Mary clung to each other. That winter, Mary grew ill with a sore throat, and no one realized for a time how sick the little girl really was. By the time Mary was better, Jennie was ill, and, in 1879, Jennie died. Both of the girls had been suffering from diphtheria.

Mary would learn to rely ever more on herself from that moment on. She had already determined that she wanted to have a career as a writer, and her mother—who was interested in forwarding the cause of women and worked extensively with organizations such as the Women's Christian Temperance Union—agreed to put Mary through Blackburn College, located in Carlinville, so that she could have a career.

Jim was already a student there when Mary started at age sixteen, and she appeared determined to outshine her older brother. Her classmates praised her compositions and poetry, and she grew ever more sure of herself while alienating others because of what she perceived as her superior intellect. However, during her first winter at Blackburn, she grew ill and was forced to return home. The following fall with her mother's approval, she enrolled at the state Normal College in Bloomington, but the curriculum for the study of becoming a teacher stifled Mary's creative impulses, and she was unhappy there. She suffered a nervous breakdown and returned home, where she reentered Blackburn and finished her education in two years. She chose to major in science, rather than English, but she was still determined to be a writer. Her mother failed to see the connection between science and writing, but Mary acted with considerable foresight in choosing her degree, as time would tell, for her first book was a study of natural history.

In the summer of 1887, a year before Mary's graduation from Blackburn, Jim heeded the call of the tales of wealth and prosperity to be had in California, and emigrated there, asking his family to join him when Mary finished school. Mary would have preferred that she and Susanna stay in Carlinville, or that she herself could go east to pursue her writing career, but Susanna insisted that the family move west to join Jim.

The two women and George took the train west to San Francisco, and along the way Mary gathered her impressions in a notebook. San Francisco and what it had to offer entranced her. Her cousin, George Lane, showed her around the city, taking her to restaurants and introducing her to the places where artists and writers were known to gather. Maybe she could have a writing career in the West! Too soon, however, she left San Francisco with her mother and brother on a boat that sailed to Los Angeles, then began the overland journey to the San Joaquin Valley. No place could be more different from the green hills of Illinois, but her imagination stirred at the barren landscape around her. She gained even more material for her writing during the overland journey by horse and wagon to meet Jim at his homestead. Mary had quickly appreciated the eerie beauty in all that was around her in the California desert.

Jim had filed claims in the name of himself, his mother, and his sister on 480 acres that he was sure would make their fortunes, but the reasons for the eerie beauty of the landscape were the same reasons that it was hell for the homesteader who expected to live off the land. At first, Mary and Susanna earned their living by cooking for a local rancher, and Jim and George worked with livestock. Mary was a talented cook, but with her college education and ideas of herself as an intellectual, she was drawn to the idea of teaching. While she was studying for the teacher's examination, she also stirred up much gossip about herself among the other settlers with her interest in learning as much as she could about the land around her from local Native Americans and from General Beale, a long-time settler in the area with a great deal of knowledge about the desert and its people.

Her intellectual pursuits weren't enough to sustain her through that first year, however, and she grew ill from malnutrition. When she was finally well, having treated herself by eating wild grapes that grew in the area, she took a job teaching at a school run by a man who owned a dairy, despite the fact that she failed the teachers' examination twice.

In 1890, she met Stafford Wallace Austin while teaching at the dairy. He was an educated man from a prominent family that had made its fortune, then lost it in Hawaii. He had taught school for a few years as well, but finding that the career didn't suit him, he was trying to start a fruit farming operation with his brother Frank in Inyo. Mary was thrilled that such an educated man had taken an interest in her, and the two were married in 1891.

The farming life didn't really suit either Mary or Wallace, as he was called. Her constitution wasn't fit for a rough frontier life as the bout with malnutrition had shown, and her temperament was not suited to housekeeping. Writing was her first love, and she thought Wallace understood that. His wedding gift to her had been a gold pen with a pearl handle. Still, their marriage seemed happy. Then their financial trouble started, with the failure of the fruit farm due to the lack of water. Mary urged Wallace to try teaching again, but he refused. Instead, undaunted by the failure, he went to San Francisco to meet with his brother about an irrigation operation in the Owens Valley while Mary remained in Inyo to write two stories, "The Mother of Felipe" and "The Conversion of Ah Lew Sing."

When Mary joined Wallace in San Francisco in 1892, she promptly carried her two stories to Ina Coolbrith in Oakland, a poetess of some repute who had associations with a San Francisco-based literary magazine called the *Overland Monthly*. With Ina's help and encouragement, she submitted the stories to the magazine before she and Wallace turned south once again to Inyo.

Mary was still in love with the desert landscape and with the characters of the people who settled there. They provided plenty of fodder for her imagination. She drew her inspiration from the Mexican and Indian residents of the area and the miners lured by tales of gold in the desert. She kept busy writing and planning for the birth of their first child while Wallace worked on the irrigation system. One day, however, she returned from a walk to find that their landlord had evicted them—her belongings were on the sidewalk. Mary had known that things weren't going well with the irrigation company, but she didn't know how bad it was, and Wallace wasn't even there to tell her himself. She picked up their belongings and walked until she found another situation for them where she could work for their board. There she was furious to learn from their new landlord that Wallace had turned down the chance to be the principal of the Inyo school, spurring the eviction from their home.

In September 1892, Mary went to her mother and brother's house in Bakersfield to await the birth of her child and to give herself some distance from her husband. While she was still recuperating from her difficult labor, the two stories she had carried with her to San Francisco were published.

Perhaps frightened by the news of the bankruptcy and bolstered by the double good news of his wife's publications and his new daughter, Wallace took a teaching job in the Owens Valley, and Mary, thinking that this was a fresh start, joined him there with Ruth. More difficulty was yet to come, though. Mary knew from the start that the beautiful Ruth was not like other babies, but when she was three a doctor confirmed that the girl was mentally retarded.

Wallace refused to discuss their daughter's condition, and Mary didn't know what to do with a child with such a severe disability. Her frustration grew, and Mary and Wallace separated shortly after the diagnosis. Mary took a teaching job in another Owens Valley town to support herself and Ruth. Their lodgings were squalid, and Mary, never a good housekeeper, couldn't or wouldn't find the time to improve them. Her writing suffered tremendously, but she knew that Ruth was suffering more from a mother who didn't know how to deal with her.

Neighbors were afraid that the baby was being neglected when they saw the conditions the two lived in, and they tried to help. Mary found it difficult to ask for assistance, or even to appear grateful for it when it was offered, so the neighbors found it hard to give. Eventually, and against Wallace's wishes, Mary boarded Ruth with a neighbor family who seemed able to control the little girl's tantrums and take better care of her than she could.

In 1898, Wallace and Mary reconciled and moved together to Independence, California, where Wallace had another teaching position, and Ruth, now six years old, went with them. Once there, they learned that Mary's mother, Susanna, had died in Los Angeles, where Mary's younger brother George was studying medicine. Mary had been ready to set out for a last visit when she heard the news of Susanna's death, but she stayed in Independence after hearing the news.

Mary loved the little town in the Owens Valley with its harsh desert landscape set off by towering mountains in the west, but in 1899, she did set out for Los Angeles with Ruth in tow. There she received the emotional support and intellectual stimulus she needed for her writing, meeting some of the most important literary figures in the United States at that time. When she returned home to Independence in 1900, she had found the inspiration and the knowledge she needed to write her most famous book, a collection of essays called *The Land of Little Rain,* all about her adopted desert home. Wallace built Mary and Ruth a home in Independence that Mary loved dearly and from there she was satisfied, at last, with the views out her window of the Sierra Nevada and Mount Whitney rising above the desert plain, and the knowledge that she was a writer. Mary's time in Independence was very productive, but still she was often ill, overworked, and exhausted with the care of Ruth. She wrote, traveled to stimulate her brain and creativity, and continued to meet and get influence from great literary minds, but she knew that something would have to change for her to live her literary dreams.

In January 1904, she finally placed Ruth in the care of a Santa Clara physician on a trial basis to see if prolonged influence of a professional would help the little girl, and in January 1905, Mary had Ruth committed permanently to an institution and would never see her again. It was a sad decision, and perhaps Mary felt some of the pain of the lack of closeness between her mother and herself when it was made, but it was time for her to move on. In late 1905, she got that chance when her first book was published. In *The Land of Little Rain*, her love for the desert shone like one of the stars in its deep black sky. She wrote:

> Out West, the west of the mesas and unpatented hills, there is more sky than any place in the world. It does not sit flatly on the rim of earth, but begins somewhere out in the space in which the earth is poised, hollows more, and is full of clean winey winds. There are some odors, too, that get into the blood. There is the spring smell of sage that is the warning that sap is beginning to work in a soil that looks to have none of the juices of life in it; it is the sort of smell that sets one thinking what a long furrow the plough would turn up here, the sort of smell that is the beginning of new leafage, is best at the plant's best, and leaves a pungent trail where wild cattle crop. There is the smell of sage at sundown, burning sage from campoodies and sheep camps, that travels on the thin blue wraiths of smoke; the kind of smell that gets into the hair and garments, is not much liked except upon long acquaintance, and every Paiute and shepherd smells

of it indubitably. There is the palpable smell of the bitter dust that comes up from the alkali flats at the end of the dry seasons, and the smell of rain from the wide-mouthed cañons. And last the smell of the salt grass country, which is the beginning of other things that are the end of the mesa trail.

With the publication of the book, Mary was considered an important American writer. She left Wallace and the Owens Valley to join an artist colony at Carmel, and her career took off to new heights. She and Wallace would never divorce, and she would never lose her love for the California desert, but she would become a world traveler; publish more than 30 books including her autobiography, *Earth Horizon*, and an autobiographical novel, *A Woman of Genius*; crusade for women's rights; and finally have the intellectual life she had always wanted.

In *The Land of Little Rain* she said of her beloved desert, "One hope the land may breed like qualities in her human offspring not tritely to 'try,' but to do." Mary was living proof that, in spite of, or perhaps because of, the landscape that shaped your existence, you could do anything you wanted. ❧

ISADORA DUNCAN
1877–1927

Carrying an Invisible Banner

*T*he performance had been electrifying and moving, but the Boston audience still sat quiet and benign in their comfortable and expensive seats when the last strains of Tchaikovsky's *Marche Slave* vanished above their heads. Suddenly, the dancer—who had just, in her usual way, put every wild sentiment in her heart into her steps and movements on the stage—grasped the end of one of the red scarves attached to her costume and raised it high overhead, proclaiming: "This is red! So am I! It is the color of life and vigor. You were once wild here. Don't let them tame you."

In October 1922, these words were almost more alarming to the good citizens of Boston than was the brief and shocking moment when, upon grasping the scarf and tearing it from her dancing tunic, Isadora Duncan revealed a bit more of herself than a proper woman ever should. It was almost unthinkable that a forty-five-year-old woman with a husband would ever put herself in such a position, much less reveal herself in that way, artist or not. It was definitely unthinkable that an American woman, even if she had been touring the world and living abroad since she was in her early twenties, would consider espousing the tenets of the Russian Revolution of 1917. But Isadora Duncan showed her feelings in front of the conservative Boston crowd, just as she would anywhere else in the world.

The world had come to expect wild and outrageous sentiments from this woman, who was often billed as the "barefoot dancer," but this time Isadora's manager informed her that she had to refrain from making further speeches on stage or her tour would be canceled. She responded with the same sentiments that had fueled her fiery speech and had inspired both the color of her costume and the music of her dance. When a more enthusiastic crowd in another city applauded wildly at the end of her magnificent interpretation of Tchaikovsky's masterpiece, she stepped forward where the lights illuminated her daring dress and declared, "My manager tells me that if I make any more speeches the tour is dead. Very well, the tour is dead. I will go back to Moscow where there is vodka, music, poetry and dancing. Oh, yes, and Freedom!"

Isadora Duncan claimed that she had been born to dance, and, in fact, she was probably born to offend and inspire people with equal measure. Since her birth in San Francisco in 1877, her headstrong attitudes and great talent as a dancer had directed the path of her family and had meant feast or famine for them. Isadora claimed her first memory was of being thrown from the window of a burning building into the arms of a policeman. The building was the hotel in Oakland, California, where she, her mother, two brothers, and sister were living when she was a small child. Isadora's mother was frantic; her father was not there. In an era where women barely dared raise their skirts above their ankles in public, for fear of attracting attention and causing scandal, the greatest of all scandals had hit the Catholic Duncan family—divorce.

When she told the story of her rescue from the fire, Isadora meant to show people that even her earliest days had been filled

Isadora Duncan

with the excitement that inspired her work. But rather than the fiery rescue, it was probably her parents' divorce that led Isadora into a life where she thought nothing of appearing barefoot and scantily clad on stage. Isadora's mother, Mary Isadora (Dora) Duncan, was the daughter of a prominent San Francisco family. Dora's father had started the first ferry service between San Francisco and Oakland and had served in the California legislature. From an early age Dora had a mind of her own, much like her youngest child would have. In 1869, against her parents' objections, she married Joseph Charles Duncan, an Episcopalian thirty years her senior, and already the father of four grown children from a previous marriage. After they married, the hard working but scheming Duncan convinced his new father-in-law to become president of a new bank that Duncan was forming.

Isadora's oldest brother claimed that she was born in 1878, but her other brother always claimed the year was 1877, which seems likely given additional anecdotal evidence. There is no way of knowing for sure, because Isadora's birth certificate, and those of most San Franciscans born in the city before 1906, were destroyed in the great fire and earthquake of that year. Until 1877, the probable year of Isadora's birth, Duncan's bank and his other speculative schemes seemed to be going quite well. Over the course of eight years, the Duncans had had four children, and the youngest, Isadora, would have been about five months old when troubles at the bank made their way into the Duncans' family life. Later, Isadora would write in her autobiography, *My Life*:

> Before I was born, my mother was in great agony of spirit, and in a tragic situation. She could take no food except iced oysters and iced champagne. If people ask me when I began to dance, I reply "In my mother's womb, probably as a result of the oysters and champagne—the food of Aphrodite."

Dora's great agony could have been caused by her knowledge of her husband's last feeble attempts to save the failing bank business. Her spirits could only have gotten worse when, five months after her dancing baby girl was born, the bank failed completely and Joseph Duncan fled the scene. Dora's father, when questioned, had to admit that no one but Joseph actually had any knowledge of the bank's operations—that he had been a mere figurehead and had lent nothing but an air of respectability to the day-to-day business of the financial institution. A warrant was put out for Joseph Duncan's arrest, and in the spring of 1878, Dora and her four children were forced to leave their comfortable home for what would be years of changing addresses due to unpaid bills and rent and odd jobs for the entire family.

When Isadora started school she remembered clearly being the poorest child in the classroom. The poverty that hung around her influenced the rest of her life, as did the comments from her mother's family about the man who had ruined her mother's life. A newly divorced Dora Duncan taught piano lessons and knitted hats and mittens for stores while the children were mostly unsupervised during the day. At night, however, came what was probably the most important part of Isadora's education. All four children would gather around their mother as she played the piano for them, and they each acquired a degree of ability themselves. Dora also occupied their minds by reading poetry and philosophy aloud. As a result, all four children developed a great appreciation for art, music, and literature.

Isadora's dancing career began early, growing both from her love of movement and from the need to escape poverty. She would dance for the girls in her neighborhood who had bicycles in exchange for rides on their marvelous toys. In addition, she earned pocket money by watching smaller neighborhood children and found that a wonderful way of keeping them occupied was to teach them simple dances. Eventually, all four Duncan children would teach social dancing to the tunes from their mother's piano.

Isadora claimed in her autobiography that she was around ten years old when this phase of her teaching career began, though it is more likely that she was in her early teens. As with her birth date, Isadora's true age at any given time as stated in her autobiography is somewhat suspect. At the time she was writing her book, she was in her forties and married to a man nearly twenty years younger than she and still had an extensive career on the stage ahead of her, all of which caused her to fib occasionally when confronted with direct questions. Given her predilection toward the dramatic, she was also not above changing facts to improve a story.

When she joined the Duncan family studio as a teacher, Isadora began to study the theory of a French voice teacher named François Delsarte through books and articles far beyond a ten-year-old's understanding. Delsarte certainly had success as a voice teacher—he mainly coached stage actors—but he became best known for his theories on movement as expression. He believed that natural movements, very unlike the forced technical work of ballet, were the most genuine and could be truly used to interpret music and make the listening experience richer through the addition of visual effects. Isadora was entranced by the idea and began composing dances for herself to music that had never been danced to before.

In about 1893, Joseph Duncan suddenly resurfaced and provided his estranged wife and children with a home at the corner of Sutter and Van Ness in San Francisco. The children called the house the Castle Mansion, and, compared to their cramped dwellings of recent years, it was magnificent. The yard contained a tennis court, a windmill, and a barn. Inside the house were a secret passage, enormous fireplaces, and beautiful, large rooms perfect for dancing and conducting their classes.

Unfortunately, the bounty only lasted for two years; Duncan

was forced to sell the house when another of his business schemes collapsed. The loss, however, spurred Isadora to make her first formal bid at becoming a performer on stage as a way of perfecting her art and making much needed money. She auditioned with the manager of a traveling company visiting San Francisco, dancing her own choreography to Mendelssohn's *Song Without Words*. Although the manager was not interested in what she had to offer the stage, Isadora remained convinced that there was a commercial application for her art. She persuaded her mother that her possibilities could only be realized in a place like Chicago, New York, or even Paris.

Isadora and her mother left San Francisco for Chicago in June 1895, leaving the other three Duncans behind. All of their belongings, including some old-fashioned jewelry, fit into one small, battered trunk. They had twenty-five dollars, which ran out long before Isadora got her first job dancing at a club called The Masonic Roof Garden. There, Isadora performed her beautiful piece to Mendelssohn, alternating it with "something peppery, with kicks and frills" at the manager's suggestion. In November 1895, she had earned her first job with a production company in New York, so she and Dora relocated again.

Isadora's brother Raymond and sister Elizabeth joined Isadora and Dora in New York when word came of her first engagement there with the production company. They apparently believed that the family's fortune was made at last. Her oldest brother, Augustin, joined them there eventually as well. In 1898, Isadora gave five solo concerts in New York to some critical acclaim. She was true to the principles she had studied in San Francisco; she refused to submit to the rigors of ballet, which she felt was unnatural and sacrificed meaning for the sake of displays of technique. Her costume was every bit as daring and revolutionary as her style of dance. She abandoned corsets and thick, heavy tights, and danced with bare arms and legs in a brief Grecian-style tunic or flowing robes. Victorian

New York, however, was not quite ready for Isadora Duncan, no matter how artfully she interpreted the music. She continued to teach dancing classes with her family when they arrived in New York, but when a fire destroyed the Duncans' home, they decided to move to London. Isadora's last concert in New York was panned by the critics, from costume to content.

In London and in Paris, Isadora became a grand success. She still suffered from money woes, but performing for fellow artists and wealthy patrons launched her career into unheard-of heights. She founded a school in Paris, where the six young girls who were her students became known as the Isadorables. Then came a great invitation to come to Russia to found a school to be financed by the newly installed Soviet government.

Although the school in Russia was never to be the success she dreamed it would be—largely because the government was unable to continue funding the venture—Isadora found it difficult to abandon her affection and admiration for the Russian people and for the communist system. Her tour in America, during which she danced the *Marche Slave* for indifferent audiences and incited their anger and dismay with her support of the Russian system, was intended as a fund-raiser for the financially strapped school.

Ironically, in spite of her love of simple things and her interest in the communist way of life, it may have been Isadora's love for luxury that eventually led to her death. In 1927, the idea for a self-sustaining school in Russia all but abandoned, she was in Paris when she requested a ride in a new, flashy automobile, a Bugatti. She settled into the seat ready for the ride, but the car sprang forward before she noticed that the end of her long, embroidered, red scarf had become tangled in the wheel. As the car pulled away from the curb, the scarf tightened around her throat, breaking her neck.

Isadora was only forty-five years old at the time of her tragic death. She had still been performing on stage, and her classes in the Duncan method had reached thousands of students. Some of her original students, the Isadorables, took her last name and taught her methods for years to come. Although her greatest dances can no longer be seen today, the power of her art is revealed in a story told by one of her closest friends, who she met in Russia.

After a performance of the third movement of Beethoven's *Sixth Symphony*, the *Pathétique*, Ilya Ilyich Schneider went to Isadora and asked:

> "How was it that you yourself held a banner with such a heavy pole, in the third part of the Sixth Symphony?" She looked at me in surprise, and I broke off my tirade, having remembered that in reality there was nothing in her hands. But the force of her art was so great that I was not alone in seeing the heavy pole of the great flag in her hands.

Isadora Duncan is rightfully called one of the founders of modern dance. She was also perhaps one of the greatest performers of the genre ever to step barefoot on the stage. ✤

TYE LEUNG SCHULZE

1887–1972

Unbound Feet, Unfettered Heart

*A*t thirteen, Tye Leung had made up her mind, and it would change her life forever. She wouldn't marry the man her parents had chosen for her—a complete stranger who wanted her to go with him to Butte, Montana. It would be terrible to leave Chinatown, her friends, and even her family, who had tried to make her go with the old man. But her next decision would have to be to leave her family behind, at least temporarily. She would go to the Presbyterian Mission Home and ask the matron there, Donaldina Cameron, to hide her from her parents, just as so many other young Chinese girls had done in San Francisco near the turn of the century.

Tye's decision to leave home and go to the mission wasn't an unusual one; in fact, it was a choice that too many young girls in turn-of-the-century San Francisco had to make. Tye was unusual, however, and her choice would help many other girls in her position and in worse circumstances change their lives as well.

In 1901 when she left home, Tye had been living in a two-room apartment in Chinatown with her mother, father, six brothers, and one sister. Tye and her brothers and sister had been born in the United States after her parents immigrated from China, so they

LOUISE SCHULZE LEE

Charles and Tye Leung Schulze

were all U. S. citizens. Not very many Chinese families lived in this country at the time because of a law that prohibited Chinese immigrants from entering. Tye's parents had arrived before the Chinese Exclusion Act of 1882 effectively ceased what had been a growing population entering this country looking for a better life, particularly in a city they called Old Gold Mountain, San Francisco.

Before the Chinese Exclusion Act passed, most of the Chinese immigrants had been men who came to work for the railroad or in the gold mines of California. Very few families traveled together to the United States from China because it was very expensive. Sons and husbands hoped to make enough money to earn passage for their families in China to join them. It was very unusual for any Chinese women to make the trip on their own, as they were bound by the taboos of a male-dominated society that kept them from venturing out on their own. In fact, most of the Chinese women of that time who could have paid for the trip were literally bound, having had their feet painfully tied from the time they were babies to keep their feet tiny, which was intended to emphasize their beauty and gentility, but also impeded their ability to walk. Such women were unable to walk far without pain, and were seldom even seen outside of their homes without the escort of a male relative.

Tye Leung's parents were unusual, because not only had they made the trip to the United States as a couple, they had allowed their children to learn American customs, and even the girls attended school. By the time she ran away to the mission, Tye had spent six years in an American school and she was one of the few people in the United States who spoke both English and Chinese.

Tye must have known the kinds of things that other girls were escaping from when they ran away to the Presbyterian Mission Home. In addition to leaving their families to avoid marriage to strangers, some girls were trying to run away from a situation in which they were enslaved. Times were hard in China and families sometimes sold their daughters to get money for food. Many times these girls were sent to the United States to work as slaves for more wealthy Chinese families, or they were forced to work as prostitutes in Chinatown. Frequently, when these girls found out about the mission home, they would send messages to Donaldina Cameron telling her that they were in desperate need of help. On the days that they were to escape from their owners, the girls would wear yellow ribbons and the mission home's rescue team would whisk them out of a crowd during their daily errands. They also conducted raids on the brothels where they were held.

Tye Leung's skills were in great demand at the mission home because she could understand the girls and help comfort them when they arrived, frightened and unable to communicate with their rescuers. In time, Tye Leung went along with the rescue teams on their crusades, working as an interpreter. It was a dangerous job, but she was proud of her work. She was helping girls who were worse off get their freedom, just as she had gotten hers.

In 1910, Tye's skills were noticed by the matron at the new immigration station in San Francisco Bay at Angel Island. Like Ellis Island in New York Harbor, Angel Island served as a checkpoint for immigrants. Many of the people who tried to pass through Angel Island made it through without difficulty, but because of the Chinese Exclusion Act, the Chinese were detained there for weeks, months, and even years while trying to gain entry into the country. They were housed in uncomfortable barracks surrounded by barbed wire and were forced to go through intense interrogations. All the while, just across the bay, their families waited for them, but no relatives were allowed on the island. Many of the missionaries who worked there tried to provide comfort and solace for the immigrants, but the language barrier was a major obstacle. Clearly, someone with Tye Leung's skills was needed at the station.

Tye worked as an assistant to the missionaries who ran the

station and as an interpreter. She was able to help and reassure hundreds of Chinese women and children who were alone in the country without money or help of any kind, and were trapped on the island. In this job, Tye became the first Chinese-American woman to work as a civil servant for the United States government.

In 1912, Tye made history again when she became the first Chinese-American woman in the United States to vote in an election. Although the law allowing women the right to vote throughout the country was not passed until 1920, California women were allowed the right in 1911. Along with two other Chinese-American women, Clara Lee and Emma Tom Leong, Tye Leung exercised that right in the face of tremendous publicity. People interested in the rights of women and of the Chinese, wanted to draw attention to the smart, pretty young women who were trying to make a difference by casting their vote. A picture of Tye behind the wheel of a Studebaker-Flanders 20 car ran in the newspaper to show that Tye was a progressive believer in the vote and in modern conveniences. In fact, she never owned a car, but the picture would do a lot to further the thinking of the modern Chinese woman toward voting and independence.

After the historic election and while she was still working as an assistant and interpreter at Angel Island, Tye met an American man named Charles Frederick Schulze. He was an immigration inspector, and the two fell deeply in love. Their parents were strongly opposed to the two marrying, and there was also a law in California from 1840–1948 that prohibited people of different races from marrying. The two decided that nothing would stop them, and they headed north to Vancouver, Washington, for the ceremony. Tye would later remember, "His mother and my folks disapprove very much, but when two people are in love, they don't think of the future or what [might] happen."

When they returned to San Francisco, which was, after all, their home, both Tye and Charles were forced to resign from the jobs because of their coworkers' strong feelings against the marriage. They also found that neither the white community nor the Chinese community was ready to accept them as a couple, and they were socially outcast.

Charles went to work as a mechanic for the Southern Pacific railroad, while Tye got a night job as a telephone operator at the Chinese telephone company. The couple lived near Chinatown and had four children, who later remembered that their parents were one of only a few interracial couples in the area. Indeed, sometimes their children were called *fan gwai jai* by their Chinese neighbors, which meant "foreign devil child." Still, Tye made a place for them in the community. Her unceasing volunteer work as an interpreter in hospitals and wherever else she was needed was enough to gain them acceptance in the Chinese community.

Charles and Tye lived a very happy life together in spite of the troubles they faced as a couple. Both of them were very independent and they each kept up their own interests, while sharing them with each other. Tye remained active in the Chinese Presbyterian Church, while Charles attended Grace Cathedral. Both loved music, and Tye spent hours playing the piano and an instrument called the Chinese butterfly harp, while Charles played French horn with a military band. The children would accompany Tye to weddings, birthday celebrations, and the Chinese opera, where they learned about their mother's culture, and they were sent to school where they learned American customs. On Sundays, the Schulzes had family time, and they made it clear that both sides of the family were to be respected and experienced with fun and joy.

Tye and Charles' marriage was unusual for many reasons, but the most important for Tye was that she was able to keep up her own interests because Charles didn't expect her to take on the traditional role of a Chinese wife. Had Tye married the Chinese man her parents had chosen for her in Butte, Montana, she would undoubtedly have been expected to stay home and care for the house and the children, and not to have a life of her own, and certainly not to have any help from her husband. Although Tye did most of the cooking and cleaning in the Schulze home, Charles stayed home with the children and cooked and cleaned for them when she was at work. He also cared for his aging mother, who lived with them.

When Tye died at the age of eighty-four in Chinatown, she was a beloved figure, who had done much to help her neighbors and to forward the rights of the Chinese people. She may never have been aware of how much she did, starting with the day she ran away to Donaldina Cameron and refused to succumb to the tradition that just a few years before would have bound her feet and her heart. ✿

MARY PICKFORD

1893–1979

United Artists' Sweetheart

*W*hen the crowds thinned at their mother's East Saint
Louis confectionery, the two little girls would slip into the nickelodeon next door with their special treat of a candied orange on a
stick and while away the afternoon watching the "flickers" that were
the specialty of these early movie theaters. One afternoon, when the
silent black-and-white scenes began to jerkily dance on the white
sheet that passed for a screen, they saw a girl who looked strangely
familiar. In *Lena and the Swan*, Lena, a Dutch peasant girl, was played
by a pretty girl with masses of curls.

As they sat in the dark in the nickelodeon, Dorothy said to her
sister, Lillian, "Look there's Gladys Smith!"

For fifteen minutes the little girls sat fascinated while their
playmate from New York City appeared on the screen, then they
rushed next door to tell their mother what they had seen. She was
surprised at the news and at first didn't believe the girls, but at last
was persuaded to go next door and see for herself. When she witnessed the little girl they had known in New York on the screen, she
said, "The Smiths must be having a difficult time of it to allow

Gladys to appear in movies. We must look them up when we get to New York. It will be good to see them again."

It was a turning point in the lives of the little Gish sisters, already fans of the new medium of movies, and who would soon be appearing in the flickers themselves. They had also witnessed the results of a major turning point in little Gladys Smith's life. When they returned to New York, they inquired about their friend Gladys at the Biograph motion picture studios and were told that the girl they were looking for was now called Mary Pickford. Gladys was already a star with Biograph, and she got jobs there for her friends Dorothy and Lillian, but bigger things, much bigger, were ahead of all of them—especially Gladys.

Gladys Smith was born in 1893 in Toronto, Ontario, Canada, the same year that Thomas Alva Edison and an assistant perfected the process of capturing motion on screen and a short film called *The Sneeze* caused audiences to exclaim loudly at its wonder. Times were hard in Toronto, so the Smiths were probably unaware of the new developments in the world of entertainment, and certainly had no thought of the impact they would eventually have on their lives. Gladys was followed by a sister, Lottie, and a brother, Jack, and their young lives would become measurably more difficult when their father died at the age of twenty-seven. Gladys was not quite five years old, but she was soon to become the family's main breadwinner.

Charlotte Smith, the children's mother, worked very hard as a seamstress to keep her little brood afloat, and she also took in boarders. For a long time, only single women rented out the large room at the front of the Smith's house, but Charlotte finally agreed to rent it to a married couple involved with a theater company. One night, the husband asked Charlotte if her daughters would be able to appear as extras in a schoolroom scene. Charlotte objected at first, but was at last persuaded that not all actresses and actors were degenerates who smoked cigarettes. Gladys and Lottie began appearing in the

Mary Pickford

play *The Silver King*, and at the age of five, Gladys began earning $10 a week.

She wasted no time stealing her first scene. With a bit of improvisation that would come in handy in the early days of motion pictures, little Gladys built a tower of blocks in one scene where she was supposed to be playing quietly while an actor and actress had a heated discussion. At a critical moment, she set the tower tumbling with a loud crash, totally disrupting the scene. She caught the director's attention, who predicted that with her beautiful, long, golden curls and talent for getting attention, she would be a star.

Shortly thereafter, Charlotte began allowing her children to appear in vaudeville shows and in other plays, and Gladys began to take on more important roles. She was famous for her winning little-girl looks and for her masses of golden curls which Charlotte, the original stage mother, fussed over constantly. They knew that the future of the theater was in New York City, so the family headed there for bigger stages in 1901.

In New York, so much was going on in the city's many theaters or with touring shows that no one went without work for long. Baby Gladys Smith, as she was billed, was becoming a star, and the marquees and reviews exclaimed, "Baby Gladys Smith is a wonder!" But with all of her commercial success, as she got older, she began to feel that there was still more to be had as an actress than lurid off-Broadway melodramas where she played a poor waif or a child in danger, so she set her sights on Broadway, and its most famous producer, former playwright David Belasco. It was 1906, she was thirteen years old, and she had made up her mind that she would stop acting if Broadway didn't want her.

When she was able to finagle an audition, she performed a scene from one of the melodramas and was cast on the spot as one of the two children in a play called *The Warrens of Virginia*. However, Belasco said, her name would not do; combining aspects of names from her family, he re-christened her Mary Pickford. As a Belasco actress on Broadway, Mary had arrived, and she wrote to her mother, then visiting Toronto with Lottie and Jack,

"GLADYS SMITH NOW MARY PICKFORD ENGAGED BY DAVID BELASCO TO PLAY ON BROADWAY THIS FALL."

Lottie and Jack quickly changed their last names to Pickford, as well, and returned to New York to capitalize on Mary's success. Mary was making $25 a week, and she played with *The Warrens of Virginia* for two years. To return to the sort of melodramatic fare she had been traveling with and appearing off-Broadway was unthinkable, but the jobs didn't always come as quickly or as often as they needed to.

In 1909 Charlotte pushed Mary into applying for work at the Biograph company in New York City. Biograph director D.W. Griffith was making silent films of the kind that were being shown across the country in nickelodeons, so called because of the five-cent ticket price. Mary was unenthusiastic about leaving Broadway and taking what was considered a big step down by appearing in motion pictures, but the new medium would make Mary known to people around the country. The flickers shown in the nickelodeons reached more people than any other form of entertainment because there was no language barrier to keep immigrants away and the price was right for almost any income.

The five-dollar-a-day pay guaranteed to motion picture actors in those days was enough to make Mary swallow her pride. Soon she found herself in the brownstone mansion that was home to Biograph appearing before David Wark Griffith. At first he told her she was too little and too fat at fifteen to appear on camera. Yet, somehow won over by her tales of experience and her pretty face and beautiful curls, he agreed to give her a screen test. She appeared with other actors carrying a mandolin and improvising dialogue. She insisted afterward that as a Broadway actress she was worth even more than the going rate and was hired at an exorbitant rate of $25 for the first three days she worked on a film and then $5 each for the remaining three days.

Mary's first movie was *Her First Biscuits*, a seven-minute farce about a new bride who wants to be a good cook. In the movie, Mary played a ten-year-old girl, for even at sixteen, she was small. Many more movies followed in which she played the lead, for she had a star quality on screen. But Mary still had some disdain for the movies, and she longed to go back to the theater. In 1912, she asked David Belasco for a chance to appear on Broadway again. He gave her the role, at age nineteen, of a twelve-year-old blind girl in a play called *A Good Little Devil*. Mary was excellent in the role; the part of a young girl suited her tiny frame and blond curls. She also memorized the stage so that she would be able to walk around without looking at anything, to appear to be truly blind.

One of the admirers of the play, and of Mary, was a man named Adolph Zukor. Zukor was a wealthy Hungarian immigrant who owned a number of nickelodeons and wanted to start a movie company of his own. The Famous Players company, which would eventually become known as Paramount, would be an assembly of some of the finest actors and actresses in New York. Mary would be one of them. Zukor caught her at a good time; he told her he would pay her five hundred dollars a week at a time when she had made up her mind to be paid that much by her imminent twentieth birthday.

During her first years back in the movies, most of Zukor's Famous Players films were made in New York City, though Mary had been to California with the company to film a number of pictures. However, it was becoming more and more clear that California was the land of promise for the burgeoning film industry. When Famous Players moved permanently to Hollywood where enormous studios were being built in the suburb amidst the lemon groves, Mary went with them. She was immediately recognized as the biggest star there, and her salary was the highest of any actor or actress in the movies. Zukor eventually gave the little girl who wanted $500 a week by the time she was twenty, a whopping $10,000-per-week salary.

The only two actors in Hollywood who were in serious competition with Mary for the role of top star were Charlie Chaplin and Douglas Fairbanks. Charlie was a relative newcomer to film; he started in 1912, three years after Mary. Douglas was an amateur with some Broadway experience whose acrobatics propelled him to stardom in films like *Zorro!* and *Robin Hood*. Mary was determined to stay ahead of Chaplin in terms of her pay—he was the second-highest paid star in the business. Douglas, on the other hand, was soon to become much more than a rival.

Early in her career with Biograph Pictures in New York City, Mary had met and fallen in love with a dashing young man named Owen Moore, and against her mother's wishes had eloped with him. Their marriage was not much more than a farce. Mary was willing to rebel enough to marry someone her mother didn't approve of, but she was still enough of a mama's girl that Charlotte called all the shots, and most of the shots had Owen out of the frame. Their marriage was essentially over when Mary went to Hollywood, and when she met the far more dashing but also married Douglas Fairbanks, the two began their long affair. Close friends and acquaintances were aware of the dalliance, but said nothing. Mary's public would never have believed it; she had made such a name for herself as the lovable young schoolgirl or orphan, rarely playing any character above sixteen years of age. She continued to soar as a star, and by now was billed everywhere as America's Sweetheart.

Perhaps Douglas's wife didn't believe it either, but their marriage was over soon after Douglas met Mary. He divorced his wife in 1918, and it was Mary's turn to divorce Owen in 1919. Mary, like other movie stars at the time, set up a temporary residence in Nevada, famous for its lenient divorce laws, where the decree was granted in March 1920. On March 28 of that year, in the Beverly Hills house that came to be known as Pickfair and was Douglas's gift to Mary, the two married after an elegant dinner party with a few guests who happened to include a minister and the Los Angeles County marriage license clerk. With their assistance, Mary and Douglas became, officially, the first couple of Hollywood.

To their fans, the alliance was natural and understandable, the symbol of clean-living American manhood had won the girl who had come to be billed as America's Sweetheart. Douglas, however, would say, "This 'America's Sweetheart' business must stop. She's my sweetheart."

The years leading into the 1920s had been Mary's golden age in movies, where she earned her title as America's Sweetheart and became, in reality, the queen of Hollywood before marrying its king. She created some of her most memorable roles, her famous curls glowing on her back even in the days of black-and-white film, while working for Famous Players under Zukor's direction. *A Little Princess*, *The Poor Little Rich Girl*, and *Rebecca of Sunnybrook Farm* helped to define her niche even further. The public wanted to see her as a little girl, and she fulfilled their wishes well into the 1920s, though in reality she was a grown woman with a husband and a keen business sense. When an actual little girl getting on a train spotted Mary wearing long fingernails and said to her mother that Mary wasn't a little girl at all, but a grown woman, Mary promptly had her nails cut short. Mary was as young as she wanted to be on stage and off. A tiny woman, only a bit over five feet, she appeared as a teenager in public and a child on screen.

Not many people knew about the shrewd businesswoman with an insatiable desire for success who hid under the famous curls. When Zukor was unable to meet her ever growing demands for control and remuneration, she had set herself up as an independent producer in November 1918 and signed a contract with a movie company called First National to distribute the films she made on her own. With this deal, her basic salary jumped to $350,000 per picture. She was twenty-six years old.

The first film Mary made on her own was based on the book *Daddy Long Legs* by Jean Webster. It was a typical role for Mary, an orphan who grows up to be a well-known writer. The next film she made was even more typical—the glad girl, Pollyanna, in the movie of the same name. With the phenomenal success of these films, Mary became fabulously wealthy. To become more wealthy still, she joined with Charlie Chaplin, Douglas Fairbanks (shortly before their marriage), and her old friend from Biograph, David Wark Griffith, to form the aptly named company, United Artists. With their new production company, the four made good pictures and good money.

Understandably, Mary grew weary of the little girl roles she felt compelled to play and the fashions she had to wear to maintain the illusion of her youth, but still she played roles like Little Lord Fauntleroy, that showcased the golden curls. The true spearhead behind United Artists and the wife of Hollywood's most dashing actor, Mary must have chafed at the roles she felt compelled to accept and at the dowdy look she was supposed to sport at his side in order to maintain her illusion. Big things were happening in the post-war world of the 1920s. Flappers were in vogue and bobbed hair was the rage. She attempted two adult roles, but they were flops at the box office. In 1925, a thirty-two-year-old Mary asked her public, through *Photoplay* magazine, what roles they would most like to see her in. *Cinderella, Anne of Green Gables, Alice in Wonderland*, and *Heidi* were the winners.

She wasn't to make any of those films, for her last role as a little girl came in 1924 when she played *Little Annie Rooney*, a motherless twelve-year-old whose policeman father dies on his birthday.

The real children hired to play in the film wouldn't fight with her as they were supposed to because she was a grown-up—and the studio head to boot. Mary finally, if slowly, moved away from those roles. Her next on-screen appearance was as a fifteen-year-old, but she didn't enjoy the success she'd had when she played younger children.

In the 1920s, another big change to the world, but especially to the motion picture industry, was in the works. Before the 1920s, all movies had been silent, accompanied only by the piano in each theater or nickelodeon. Now, experiments were being made with sound, and in 1927, Al Jolson spoke the first words on screen in *The Jazz Singer.* In 1928 a newcomer to the Hollywood scene, Walt Disney, produced the first animated film with sound, *Steamboat Willie.* The world was forever changed.

Mary's last silent film, made in 1927, was *My Best Girl.* She played a twenty-year-old girl working as a clerk in a five-and-dime store who meets the son of the owner of the chain and falls in love. Her costar was Buddy Rogers, and the film featured two firsts in Mary's career. She wore the famous Pickford curls on top of her head instead of cascading down her back, and she had her first on-screen kiss. The movie was one of her best, and it seemed to mark the point of no return.

Mary took a year off from films after the release of *My Best Girl,* which was a phenomenal success, and it must have been a soul-searching year. On June 21, 1928, while in New York City after a trip to Europe with Douglas, she went to the salon of Charles Bock to have the curls removed. Her fans, and her husband, were some-what aghast at the news of one of the most publicized haircuts in history. Mary later said:

> You would have thought I murdered someone, and per-haps I had, but only to give her successor a chance to live. It was a very sad business indeed to be made to feel that

my success depended solely, or at least in large part, on a head of hair.

I naturally missed my curls after they were gone. I had always taken care of my own hair, washed it and curled the ringlets over my fingers. But I thought that getting rid of them would free me, and I suppose in a way it did. I began to feel a change, a sense of ease and liberation that I hadn't known before. It was my final revolt against the kind of role I had been playing.

The break was complete, and with her next film, she demonstrated it. In 1928, she performed in *Coquette*, playing a 1920s vamp with bobbed hair, short skirts, and dangerous silk stockings. She was Norma Bessant, a girl torn between her father and her illicit lover—a dramatic departure from the golden-haired child roles she had been playing. In the movie, Norma's father was forced to kill the lover and then himself. *Coquette* was also Mary's first film with sound, and the critically acclaimed performance won her an Oscar in April 1929, the second year that the awards were given. Mary had grown up and, in her own way of thinking, she had finally arrived.

During the time that *My Best Girl* and *Coquette* were being filmed, a break of another kind was occurring in Mary's life. She and Doug, the leading couple in Hollywood who had appeared totally devoted to one another in public and in private for the last eight years, were nearing the breakup of their marriage.

In 1929, they made their first and only film together, *The Taming of the Shrew*, to some critical success. Mary, however, felt that her performance in the role of Katherine was her worst ever. Her confidence was shattered, and failed films in 1930, 1931, and 1932 led to her belief in 1933 that it was time to retire from films. Doug was also having problems with his career. It was difficult for him to make the transition to the "talkies," as they were called, and the melodramatic action films that were his trademark didn't play as well to audiences when his acrobatic stunts were accompanied by sound.

Friends were startled to notice that in 1931, Doug began spending more time away from Mary, when they used to be inseparable. He was seen often in the company of Lady Sylvia Ashley, a former model and chorus girl, twenty years his junior, and now the wife of Lord Ashley. In January 1934, Ashley divorced his errant wife, and in December of that same year, Mary filed for divorce from Doug, and in January 1935, the decree was granted in spite of pleas from the public and from Doug himself.

Throughout the thirties, Mary remained busy as a Hollywood producer and with her work at United Artists. Doug was also involved with United Artists, so the two remained in contact, in spite of his marriage to Sylvia Ashley. Mary remained at Pickfair and, in 1937, married Buddy Rogers—ten years after filming of *My Best Girl* with him. However, Mary was really in love with Doug for the rest of her life. When he died on December 12, 1939, she was grief stricken. It seems that one of his last thoughts was of her; before his death, he sent a message to her by way of his brother.

Throughout the forties, Buddy and Mary appeared to have a happy family life, adopting two children, and living and entertaining in Pickfair frequently. Mary remained involved in the movie business as a producer and could only laugh when she was named on a list of "has-beens" in *Life* magazine, along with fifteen-year-old Shirley Temple, who had revived many of Mary's roles as a child actress. When rumors went around that Mary was thinking of suing the magazine, she said, "Stuff and nonsense. Nothing could be further from the truth. As a matter of fact I enjoyed the picture and was highly amused by the caption. How could I resent being labeled a 'has-been' when I am placed in the same division as a junior miss of fifteen?"

But it was the beginning of the end for Mary. Though she was involved in civic affairs and in the movie world into the fifties, enough became enough. In 1956, she sold her remaining shares in United Artists but continued to make public appearances. In 1977, she received the Lifetime Achievement Award from the Academy of Motion Picture Arts and Sciences, but by and large she remained secluded in Pickfair with Buddy nearby and her favorite mementos on the wall. She died in the Santa Monica hospital after a short illness on May 29, 1979, at the age of 87.

Doug's son from his first marriage, Douglas Fairbanks, Jr., eulogized his stepmother, with whom he had remained close over the years:

> It was her idea that artists who created their own works from the beginning; who invented the stories; who defined, authorized, approved and indicated the kind of settings they wanted; who chose their directors, the kind of effects they wished to achieve. . . in other words they were not only producers who just packaged films but actually created films, and so should indeed have the rewards due to them—rather that be paid to the middleman, in other words, the big distributors . . . who were taking an undue amount of the profits."

His words summed up what was the genius of the Mary Pickford way, the United Artists way. Mary had died a wealthy woman with a legacy that was far outweighed by the legacy she left in film. She had been the most beloved woman in the world for a time, had three husbands who adored her, and was captured on film forever at the time when her public wanted to see more and more of her.

She herself summed up some of her own feelings about her phenomenal rise when in her memoirs she recalled a dinner party she gave for the king and queen of Siam in Pickfair during her marriage to Doug. The king and queen had arrived at Pickfair early to play tennis before dinner, and the queen had slipped in some mud. While the queen cleaned herself up in Mary's bathtub, she stood outside in the hallway and thought to herself, "Imagine you, Gladys Smith of Toronto, Canada, with the queen of Siam in your bathtub." Baby Gladys, a wonder then, a wonder as Mary Pickford, exemplified the California Hollywood dream. ✿

DOROTHEA LANGE

1895–1965

Life Through a Lens

*E*ven in southern California near the coast at Santa Barbara, the late winter could be raw and miserable. In March 1936, Dorothea Lange was eagerly headed north for home in the frigid air after a wet, rainy month on the road. There were rolls and rolls of exposed film safe on the seat of the car beside her, and she was anxious for the comforts of home and to see her husband after this field trip.

On the side of the road near Nipomo, Dorothea saw a sign—just a simple sign like so many others—out of the corner of her eye. "Pea-Pickers Camp," it said. She didn't stop, or even slow the car, but twenty miles farther up the road, she made a U-turn and headed back.

She didn't really know why. She already had plenty of photos of migrant workers in California's produce fields and orchards. The Great Depression of the 1930s and the dust bowl conditions in the southern Midwest had driven many farmers from their homes to pick for more prosperous operations in the West. Even in California, long known as the land of plenty, work was hard to come by.

Dorothea Lange

Dorothea Lange was a documentary photographer—almost before anyone knew what that was—who recorded the plight of the migrant worker in order to illustrate their need for assistance in magazines, newspapers, and other publications of the day. She had learned to capture the stories of the migrants with pathos and dignity, and when she turned around to go back toward the pea-pickers camp, one of her greatest images of the era was ahead of her.

She later said about that day, "I was following instinct, not reason. I drove into that wet and soggy camp and parked my car like a homing pigeon."

Her instincts led her to a mother and her children who were desperately hungry and cold, and of whom she took five photos, working her way closer and closer to her subjects as she asked them about themselves. She later recalled:

> I saw and approached the hungry and desperate mother, as if drawn by a magnet. I did not ask her name or history. She told me her age, that she was thirty-two. She said they had been living on frozen vegetables from the surrounding fields, and birds that the children killed. She had just sold the tires from her car to buy food. There she sat in that lean-to tent with her children huddled around her, and seemed to know that my pictures might help her, and so she helped me. There was a sort of equality about it.

As soon as Dorothea returned home to Berkeley, California, she developed the film and rushed the prints to a San Francisco newspaper editor. The paper reported the story—illustrated by Dorothea's photographs—of the 2,500 migrant workers who, like the young mother, were stranded and hungry because of crop failure. The federal government responded to it with 20,000 pounds of food.

Migrant Mother, Nipomo, California, 1936
Photo by Dorothea Lange

DOROTHEA LANGE

As a child, Dorothea Nutzhorn had walked nearly a mile to school every day through an area of Hoboken, New Jersey known as the Thieves' Highway. At the age of twelve, she became accustomed to stepping over drunks on the sidewalk and trying not to show how scared she was of the petty thieves selling goods along the way.

Her grandparents had all come to the United States from Germany looking for a better life. They settled in Hoboken, where the Nutzhorn's son, Henry, a lawyer, married Joan, the librarian daughter of the Langes. Dorothea was born to these happy parents on May 25, 1895. The young family moved to several New Jersey towns, landing back in Hoboken.

When Dorothea was seven, she contracted polio, which damaged her right leg from the knee down. Other children called her "Limpy," and even her mother seemed embarrassed by her daughter's bad leg, asking her to walk better when they approached friends on the street. Still, Dorothea loved her mother very much, even if she thought she should pay less attention to what the neighbors thought.

When she was small, Dorothea's father read Shakespeare to her and took her to see a performance of *A Midsummer Night's Dream* when she was ten. He took her to the play in a coach and when there were no tickets left, he held her on his shoulders at the back of the crowded theater so that she could enjoy the show. Then, when Dorothea was twelve, her father left his family and she never saw him again. The loss devastated her.

Joan Lange Nutzhorn and Dorothea moved in with her mother Sophie and Aunt Caroline in Hoboken. Sophie was a talented dressmaker with a terrible temper. While Dorothea was in high school—a miserable time for the girl who excelled in the arts but not much else and was different from her classmates because of her limp and her family situation—Grandmother Sophie began drinking too much and frequently quarreled with Dorothea. Great-Aunt Caroline was a comfort, but still Dorothea stayed away from the house as much as possible.

Dorothea had one friend, Florence, called Fronsie, who joined her in skipping classes to go to plays, art shows, museums, and Central Park. Still, Dorothea managed to graduate, and when her mother—who wanted her daughter to go to college to become a teacher, one of the only acceptable professions for women at the time—asked her what she wanted to do, Dorothea knew. Even though she had never even held a camera, she said, "I want to be a photographer."

Joan was surprised and dismayed by her daughter's announcement, and she insisted that Dorothea go to a teacher-training program in New York. Dorothea wasn't enthusiastic about her studies, but she obeyed her mother. One day, however, as she walked down Fifth Avenue she noticed a window with portrait photographs by Arnold Genthe. Boldly, she walked into his studio and asked for a job. Genthe was one of the greatest photographers in the United States; he had taken photos of presidents, actors, writers, opera singers, and other famous personages. He was also famous for his photographs of the great earthquake of 1906 in San Francisco.

Much to her surprise, and perhaps to his, Genthe hired the young woman on the spot. For a time, Dorothea continued her teacher training while learning the art of photography, but when school was out at three o'clock, she would hurry to the studio where she printed proofs, retouched negatives, and mounted and framed photographs. She also learned from Genthe's artistry. He had the ability to bring out the personality and character of even the plainest person in his portraits.

Dorothea also learned from Genthe what it was like to work at something you truly loved. She dropped out of school and spent six months at another portrait studio, where she learned how to run a photography business and got her first big break. She later said, "It was the first big job I ever did. I was scared to death I wouldn't be able to do acceptable pictures."

The subject on that first job was the wealthy Brokaw family, and they were so pleased with her work that word spread throughout New York's wealthy families about Dorothea. Her boss made her the chief photographer at the studio.

Even though she was having so much success, Dorothea still considered herself an apprentice, and she tried to learn everything she could from each photographer she met. Eventually, with the help of a photographer who taught her how to set up a darkroom in the chicken shed at her mother's home in exchange for using it, Dorothea started her own studio. Her mother now went proudly about saying, "My daughter is a photographer."

In 1918, Dorothea, at twenty-three, decided to travel around the world with her good friend Fronsie, who had become a Western Union telegraph operator. Dorothea felt sure that she could make her living from her camera as they traveled, and Fronsie's boss told her that she could have a job with Western Union in any city in the world.

The two young women left with about $140 and one suitcase between them. They traveled across the United States and ended up in San Francisco. When they arrived in the bustling city on the bay, they were robbed, and their trip was cut short. It was a major change in Dorothea's plans, but she decided to stay put and start over with a photography job in San Francisco. She started over in another way, too: She dropped her long-absent father's last name and became officially known as Dorothea Lange.

Dorothea quickly found a job at Marsh's, a camera supply store, where she processed film while taking her own photos on the side. A year later, a generous businessman, impressed with her work, helped her establish her own studio.

Once again, a good session with a wealthy family established her as the preeminent photographer of San Francisco's elite. She was soon busy night and day.

In 1920, the successful young photographer met and married a painter named Maynard Dixon. He was twenty years older than Dorothea, and both were passionately committed to their work, so it must have been hard for them to keep their marriage together. Even after the births of their two sons, Daniel and John, neither Dorothea nor Maynard was able to commit to a solid family life—both were too busy with other things they thought were more important.

Still, the market for photos and paintings was good, and both were happy with the work they produced. Then, in 1929, the stock market crashed, signaling the start of what would be known as the Great Depression. Even the wealthy stopped buying luxury items like art and portrait photographs.

With her studio quiet for the first time in years, Dorothea started walking among the people who milled in the streets outside or stood in line for bread at stations that had cropped up all over the city to feed the hungry. There seemed to be more hungry every day.

Her first photograph of the strange phenomena caused by the crash was called *White Angel Bread Line*, and it became one of her best-known images. In it she captured the suffering of men out of work, unable to feed their families, and forced to rely on charity for their bread.

Dorothea didn't know what she would do with these photographs—it didn't pay anything for her to take them, but she felt compelled to use her camera to record the events outside of the studio more and more. Labor strikes, longshoremen at work, homeless families, and field workers became her subjects.

When Franklin Delano Roosevelt was elected president in 1932, hope finally began to surface for families that had been devastated by the Depression. Roosevelt had a plan, called the New Deal, to spend federal money in creative ways to alleviate the suffering all over the country.

Jobless on Edge of Pea Field, Imperial Valley, California, 1937
Photo by Dorothea Lange

As a part of these programs, Dorothea was invited to share her photographs of the Depression in an exhibit sponsored by the government where many people would see the plight of the poor in America and come to support the president's plan to help them. Paul Taylor, a professor at the University of California at Berkeley, saw her photographs at the exhibit and asked to use them to illustrate an article he had written.

Soon, Paul and Dorothea were collaborating on many projects. She loved the way he got stories from people, and he loved the way she quietly captured what his words could never tell completely. Eventually, the two fell in love, and each divorced their spouses. They were married shortly before Dorothea's fortieth birthday.

Dorothea had found her way—as an artist who was helping people. It was shortly after her marriage to Paul that she took the photograph at the pea-pickers camp. She didn't know it, but she was forging a new path in photography, called documentary photography, and many artists who came after her would try to emulate her style and methods in illustrating the world around them. Throughout the 1930s, she and Paul were hired to work on reports for the government, and she was always praised for her skill in approaching her subjects.

Dorothea traveled all over the country documenting the years of the Great Depression, but in 1941 when the United States went to war with Japan, she got another chance to photograph the people of California for the government.

After Japan bombed Pearl Harbor on December 7, 1941, and the United States entered World War II, the government decided to intern all Japanese immigrants and citizens who lived in the United States in barbed-wire camps. Two of the largest were built in California at Tule Lake and Manzanar.

It was a terrible violation of human rights, and, strangely, the government decided to document it on film. They hired Dorothea, who, along with her husband, was an outspoken opponent of the internment. She took many striking images of the tragedy, but the government hid them away until 1972, when they were finally exhibited to the public. Even after the war ended in 1945, the government wasn't willing to take responsibility for the unfair action, and perhaps they hired Dorothea so that she would be unable to publish photographs that might have raised public opposition to the outrage of keeping innocent people behind wire.

During the time that Dorothea worked on the photos of the internment camps, she developed a stomach ulcer that required surgery. For three years her camera was put quietly away. When at last she was able to photograph again, she began taking photos she called, "Relationships." These were pictures of the everyday lives of the people and families around her. The war, the depression, and the dust bowl years were behind them. She suddenly made more time for her own relationships with her children, and now, grandchildren.

In 1964, Dorothea was told she had terminal cancer, and she said, "Just when I have gotten on the track, I find that I am going to die. There are so many things I have yet to do that it would take several lifetimes in which to do them all."

She asked the doctor how much time she had left, and in her remaining months she prepared a photographic essay called *The American Country Woman* that is one of her greatest legacies. She worked on two television films about her life and her work, and she also accepted an invitation from the Museum of Modern Art in New York to prepare a show of her life's work.

The exhibit was almost completed when she died at the age of seventy on October 11, 1965. Three months later, it opened to great acclaim. One of the most striking images was the one she took that day at the pea-pickers camp. Called *Migrant Mother*, it has appeared all over the world in books, magazines, pamphlets, newspapers, films, television, and exhibits. It is a simple photo with a simple subject. The woman touches her creased face with a work-worn hand, her ragged sleeve around her elbow. Two children bury their heads behind their mother's narrow shoulders. Dorothea's art made the simple photo a plea for help that no words could ever make. ⚜

BIBLIOGRAPHY

MARY ELLEN PLEASANT

Bennet Jr., Lerone. "The Mystery of Mary Ellen Pleasant." *Ebony.* April and May 1979.

Longstreet, Stephen. *The Wilder Shore: A History of the Gala Days of San Francisco.* Garden City, N.Y.: Doubleday, 1968.

Ravage, John W. *Black Pioneers: Images of the Black Experience on the North American Frontier.* Salt Lake City: University of Utah Press, 1997.

JESSIE BENTON FRÉMONT

Egan, Ferol. *Frémont, Explorer for a Restless Nation.* Garden City, N.Y.: Doubleday, 1977.

Morrison, Dorothy N. *Under a Strong Wind, The Adventures of Jessie Benton Frémont.* New York: Athenum, 1983.

Roske, Ralph J. *Everyman's Eden: A History of California.* New York: Macmillan, 1968.

TOBY RIDDLE

Bauer, Helen. *California Indian Days.* Garden City, N.Y.: Doubleday, 1968.

Dillon, Richard. *Burnt-Out Fires: California's Modoc Indian War.* Englewood Cliffs, N.J.: Prentice Hall, 1973.

Faulk, Odie B., and Laura E. Faulk. *The Modoc.* New York: Chelsea House Publishers, 1988.

Rawls, James J. *Indians of California: The Changing Image.* Norman, O.K.: University of Oklahoma Press, 1984

SARAH WINCHESTER

Olsen, Bobbi. "Weekend Escape: San Jose; Guns and Roses; A Bit of Supernatural Mystery, Intrigue, and Lots of Night Magic in a Town Everyone Knows the Way to." *Los Angeles Times*. 6 October 1996.

Rambo, Ralph. *Lady of Mystery*. San Diego, CA: The Rosicrucian Press, Ltd, 1967.

The Winchester Mystery House. San Jose, California: The Winchester Mystery House, 1997.

Woelfl, Genevieve. *A Driven Woman: Sarah Pardee Winchester, Her Compelling Story*. Brooklyn, N.Y.: Redwood Publishers, 1986.

FLORENCE HUTCHINGS

Kaufman, Polly Welts. *National Parks and the Woman's Voice: A History*. Albuquerque: University of New Mexico Press, 1996.

Sanborn, Margaret. *Yosemite: Its Discovery, Its Wonders and Its People*. Yosemite National Park: The Yosemite Association, 1989.

Sargent, Shirley. *Pioneers in Petticoats: Yosemite's Early Women, 1856-1900*. Yosemite, Calif.: Flying Spur Press, 1966.

MARY AUSTIN

Austin, Mary. *Earth Horizon*. Albuquerque: University of New Mexico Press, 1991.

————. *The Land of Little Rain*. Boston and New York: Houghton Mifflin, 1903.

Church, Peggy Pond. *Wind's Trail: The Early Life of Mary Austin*. Santa Fe: The Museum of New Mexico Press, 1990.

Fink, Augusta. *I-Mary: A Biography of Mary Austin*. Tucson: University of Arizona Press, 1983.

Stineman, Esther Lanigan. *Mary Austin: Song of a Maverick*. New Haven: Yale University Press, 1989.

ISADORA DUNCAN

Blair, Fredrika. *Isadora: Portrait of the Artist As a Woman*. New York: McGraw Hill, 1986.

BIBLIOGRAPHY

Duncan, Irma. *The Technique of Isadora Duncan.* New York: Kamin, 1937.

Duncan, Isadora. *My Life.* New York: Liveright, 1927.

Schneider, Ilya Ilyich, *Isadora Duncan: The Russian Years.* New York: Harcourt, Brace, and World, 1968.

TYE LEUNG SCHULZE

Goldberg, George. *East Meets West: The Story of the Chinese and Japanese in California,* New York: Harcourt, Brace, Jovanovich, 1970.

Weatherford, Doris. *Foreign and Female: Immigrant Women in America, 1840-1930.* New York: Facts on File, Inc., 1995.

Yung, Judy. *Unbound Feet: A Social History of Chinese Women in San Francisco.* Berkeley: University of California Press, 1995.

MARY PICKFORD

Eyman, Scott. *Mary Pickford, America's Sweetheart.* New York: Donald I. Fine, 1990.

Gish, Lillian, *The Movies, Mr. Griffith, and Me.* New Jersey: Prentice Hall, 1969.

Pickford, Mary. *Sunshine and Shadow.* New York: Doubleday, 1955.

Windeler, Robert. *Sweetheart: The Story of Mary Pickford.* New York: Praeger Publishers, 1973.

DOROTHEA LANGE

Dorothea Lange. New York: Museum of Modern Art, 1966.

Lange, Dorothea. *Dorothea Lange Looks at the American Country Woman.* Fort Worth, Texas: Amon Carter Museum, 1967.

Meltzer, Milton. *Dorothea Lange, Life Through the Camera.* New York: Viking Kestrel, 1985.

Ohrn, Karin Becker. *Dorothea Lange and the Documentary Tradition.* Baton Rouge: Louisiana State University Press, 1980.

INDEX